# Presentation Skills for Technical Professionals

## Achieving Excellence

Soft Skills for
IT Professionals

# Presentation Skills for Technical Professionals

## Achieving Excellence

NAOMI KARTEN

Soft Skills for
IT Professionals

IT Governance Publishing

Every possible effort has been made to ensure that the information contained in this book is accurate at the time of going to press, and the publishers and the author cannot accept responsibility for any errors or omissions, however caused. No responsibility for loss or damage occasioned to any person acting, or refraining from action, as a result of the material in this publication can be accepted by the publisher or the author.

Microsoft and PowerPoint are registered trademarks of Microsoft Corporation in the United States and/or other countries. Apple and Keynote are registered trademarks of Apple Inc.

Apart from any fair dealing for the purposes of research or private study, or criticism or review, as permitted under the Copyright, Designs and Patents Act 1988, this publication may only be reproduced, stored or transmitted, in any form, or by any means, with the prior permission in writing of the publisher or, in the case of reprographic reproduction, in accordance with the terms of licenses issued by the Copyright Licensing Agency. Enquiries concerning reproduction outside those terms should be sent to the publishers at the following address:

IT Governance Publishing
IT Governance Limited
Unit 3, Clive Court
Bartholomew's Walk
Cambridgeshire Business Park
Ely
Cambridgeshire
CB7 4EH
United Kingdom

*www.itgovernance.co.uk*

First published in the United Kingdom in 2010
by IT Governance Publishing.

ISBN: 978-1-84928-073-0

# ABOUT THE SOFT SKILLS FOR IT PROFESSIONALS SERIES

IT is often seen as a 'hard-skill' profession where there is no place for soft skills. Yet the importance of soft skills for the IT professional should not be underrated; they underlie all behaviours and interactions. Both IT and non-IT professionals need to work together and learn from each other for effective business performance. All professionals, be they in IT or elsewhere, need to understand how their actions and reactions impact on their behaviour and working relationships.

This series of books aims to provide practical guidance on a range of soft-skills areas for those in IT and also for others, including those who deal with IT professionals, in order to facilitate more effective and co-operative working practices.

Each book is written by an experienced consultant and trainer. Their approach throughout is essentially practical and direct, offering a wealth of tried and tested professional guidance. Each chapter contains focused questions to help the manager plan and steer their course. The language used is jargon-free, and a bibliography is included at the end of the book.

Angela Wilde

IT Governance

# FOREWORD

"Oh drat," you think. "I've got to do a presentation!"

Nevertheless, you smile and ask, "Oh, sure – what's the date?"

*Presentation Skills for Technical Professionals* to the rescue!

Out comes Naomi Karten's splendid book. You open it, eager for your session with your personal presentation skills coach. You are easily captivated by Naomi's clever style and practical guidance on presentations, and grateful for the online references and resources that supplement the text. Reading this book not only prepares you for your upcoming presentation, it also helps you get in the groove and enables you to gain confidence as you prepare. You actually *enjoy* the process!

I was flattered when Naomi asked me to write the foreword for her latest book. I view Naomi as one of the best technical writers on the planet. Her writing encapsulates hard-nosed wisdom and pragmatic advice in an easy, approachable style. And, Naomi is a consummate presenter with an abundance of experience speaking to technical audiences.

My first big speaking engagement at a major conference was a life-draining experience for me. I practiced until I was bored, worried for weeks, and was incredibly nervous the night before (I barely slept). It all went fine – and was life changing for me. I learned I could do it! I enjoyed the challenge and recognized that delivering presentations is essential to my personal and professional development.

But I can tell you without doubt that I would have benefited greatly from the calm wisdom in this book. Now with a few presentations under my belt, I thoroughly enjoyed reading the book to learn more from a first-rate guide.

You can read this book front to back for a holistic immersion or dive into a topic that tickles your fancies or fears, such as sections entitled *Physical mannerisms*, *How stories make facts interesting*, *Dress to unstress*, or *Speak – don't die*. With Naomi at your side, whispering wisdom and lighthearted stories in an empathetic tone, you'll find a friend in her voice, a coach in her advice, a confidant in her stories.

This book is practical, pragmatic, and a joy to read: concise, clever, captivating and compelling. It allows you to settle down, focus, find your voice and confidence; it reminds you of the undisputable humanity of your audience, yourself, and all the other wary presenters who came before. It allows you to take pride and joy in the outcome.

So free your fears, halve your heartache, unravel your uncertainties, and set your mind at ease. I can think of no better guide for a technical person seeking excellent presentation skills than Naomi Karten's *Presentation Skills for Technical Professionals*.


Ellen Gottesdiener

EBG Consulting, Inc.

# ABOUT THE AUTHOR

As a highly experienced professional speaker and seminar leader, Naomi Karten draws from her psychology and IT background to help organizations improve customer satisfaction, manage change, and strengthen communication and presentation skills. She has delivered seminars and presentations to more than 100,000 people throughout Europe, the US, and Canada, and is well-known for delivering serious material with a light touch.

Naomi's e-book, *How to Establish Service Level Agreements*, has helped organizations worldwide establish successful SLAs. Her other books and e-books include *Changing How You Manage and Communicate Change*, *Communication Gaps and How to Close Them*, *Managing Expectations*, and *How to Survive, Excel and Advance as an Introvert*.

Naomi's website, *www.nkarten.com*, features more than 100 articles on a wide range of topics, including strengthening customer relations, improving communication, gathering customer feedback, and enhancing teamwork.

Naomi's newsletter, *Perceptions & Realities*, is highly regarded for offering serious advice in a lively, chuckle-generating manner. Numerous issues of this newsletter are posted on her website. In addition, she has published more than 300 articles in print and online publications.

Before forming her training and speaking business, Naomi earned degrees in psychology and gained experience in technical, customer support, and management positions.

# ACKNOWLEDGEMENTS

I am forever grateful to all of you who have invited me to give presentations and have attended my presentations. Without you, I would never have gained the experience to write this book.

In addition, many people responded to my request for input. Thank you for taking the time, providing valuable information, and sharing my enthusiasm for this book: Szifra Birke, Eric Bloom, Carol Brumwell, Miquel Casas, Fiona Charles, Jutta Eckstein, Andre Gous, Payson Hall, Francesco Ientile, Kim Laursen, and Johanna Rothman.

Numerous other people became contributors to this book when they made a comment, told me a story, or described an experience that, unknown to them, was exactly what I was writing about. Thank you for giving permission to use your comments: Rex Andre, Selena Delesie, Dale Emery, Tobias Fors, Judith Marx Golub, Sherry Heinze, Neil Lapham, Rob Peck, Jude Rajan, Lou Russell, Jeff Switzer, and Becky Winant.

And several people eagerly and graciously reviewed parts of the book and gave me invaluable feedback. Thank you, Roy Atkinson, Szifra Birke, Fiona Charles, Sherry Heinze, Helen Osborne, Adrian Segar, Greg Stoltz, Shannon Stoltz, and Becky Winant. Each of you provided suggestions that I immediately applied.

Finally, thank you, Mark Tatro, my favorite illustrator (*www.rotategraphics.com*), for cartoons that capture the whimsical side of public speaking.

# CONTENTS

# Contents

# Contents

# Contents

# Contents

# Contents

# Contents

# INTRODUCTION: PLEASE JOIN ME IN WELCOMING …

You're the featured presenter at today's meeting. Your stomach is in knots. It's 15 minutes to start time. You teeter to the front of the room. Your heart is pounding. You set up your material, nearly tripping over a cord. People begin to arrive. You turn away so they can't see you quivering and quaking. Ten minutes to go. Your hands are shaking and sweaty. *Never again*, you tell yourself. Seven minutes left. The room is packed. You feel wobbly. Five minutes to go. Your throat tightens up. Four minutes. You can't breathe. Three. You're certain you're going to die. Two …

Oops, wrong opening. Wait, here's the right one …

You're the featured presenter at today's meeting. Confidently, you stride into the room. You arrange your material, comfortable that you've checked all the details in advance. As people arrive, you greet them, shake hands, chat. You've prepared for this presentation and you're excited about giving it. Time to start. You take a deep breath, make eye contact with several audience members, and begin. People listen attentively. They nod, they laugh, they absorb your well-crafted material. They ask questions; you answer them. You summarize your key points and end on time. The audience is appreciative. You presented useful information in an engaging manner.

If this is what you're striving for as a presenter, this book will help you achieve it.

## What's in it for you?

Some technical professionals are excellent presenters. Whether through training, feedback, experience, or an intuitive grasp of how to do it, they're good at it. If this describes you, I applaud you. As a population, however, technical professionals aren't known for having the greatest presentation skills.

Nevertheless, the ability to give a presentation to your customers at a project review meeting, your peers in a webinar, or an audience of managers and techies at a conference can significantly boost your credibility, clout, and professional status. Delivering a presentation at work, or at professional events, is an opportunity to share your insights, convey important information, and gain a reputation as an expert in your topic.

Being known as an accomplished presenter is an unbeatable career credential. Whether your career follows a technical, business, or management track, or something else altogether, presentation skills will help you accomplish more – and be more valued for what you accomplish. Whether or not you're interested in giving formal presentations, the ability to present will boost your communication, persuasion, and leadership skills.

## Naomi as a formerly panicked speaker

I resent TV testimonials of the *if I can do it, so can you* variety. Just because one person succeeded in a particular challenge doesn't mean anyone else can do the same. Nevertheless, I want to make a similar claim about presenting: if I could learn to do it, so can you. If I was able to overcome the fear of public speaking, so can you. If I could develop strong presentation skills, so can you. I say this with certainty because no one was less likely than I was to become a public speaker, and indeed, a professional speaker.

I still remember, oh so clearly, what it was like to be terrified of public speaking – or rather, the *prospect* of public speaking, since I was determined never to actually do it. In fact, finding ways to *avoid* giving presentations was a high priority. When I was an IT project manager, my company offered presentation skills classes. One person per department could attend the class. Each time the class was offered, I made sure someone from the department took it. It'll be good training for you, I told them.

What I really meant was "If you attend, I won't have to." Me? I wanted nothing to do with public speaking.

When notices of the class continued to come around after everyone else in the department had attended, I sent each of them again. It'll be a good refresher, I told them. What I really meant was "If you attend, I won't have to."

But having spent years in technical positions, I was in line to become a department manager. That meant that eventually, like it or not, I'd have to give presentations. Not wanting to make a total fool of myself presenting to our customers or the IT vice president, I figured I'd better get some training. In my first classroom presentation, I learned the meaning of the phrase "my heart was in my throat." My presentation was only two minutes long, but my heart was pounding so hard, I thought it would bounce off the classroom walls.

After giving several presentations to my equally nervous classmates, the thumpety-thumping of my heart decreased to a minor thud-thud-thud. In subsequent courses, I learned that I had useful ideas to offer and that I could be funny in front of an audience. I also learned that people view me as an energetic speaker. (As an introvert, I love that!)

As luck would have it, I spent several years as a manager without having to give anything more than brief presentations at project rollouts and management meetings. But as soon as I formed my training and consulting business, I started receiving invitations to speak at conferences. As I prepared for them, I bounced back and forth between sheer panic – *I can't do it!* – and certainty that I'd do it, and survive doing it.

The latter turned out to be correct. Despite my inexperience, I did reasonably well. More importantly, I discovered that I enjoyed presenting. Speaking and training became the core of my business.

Though I could never have anticipated it, I became a professional speaker. Companies began to hire me to speak at their events and give seminars to their technical and non-technical staff. Soon, I was speaking internationally. Even now, more than 20 years after my first public presentation, I scratch my head and ponder how I, of all people, could have become a professional speaker.

## Thus, this book

Thanks to the opportunities I've had to become a confident and experienced presenter, I'm eager to help you improve *your* confidence and competence as a presenter.

Here's what this book addresses:

**Part I, Becoming a skilled presenter**, sets the stage. Chapter 1 provides a quick overview of the essentials, things to keep in mind if you don't have time to read an entire book before your next presentation. Chapter 2 helps you find your voice as a presenter. Chapter 3 describes the attributes of good and bad presentations. Chapter 4 discusses presentation anxiety, something most presenters are familiar with.

**Part II, Developing engaging content**, guides you in developing your presentation. Chapter 5 focuses on key steps in shaping your presentation. Chapters 6 to 9 describe important aspects of preparing your presentation, including creating a strong opening and closing, incorporating interaction, telling stories, and creating effective slides.

**Part III, Preparing to present**, stresses that *creating* a great presentation is no assurance that you'll *give* a great presentation – unless you've prepared. To that end, Chapter 10 describes key logistical issues to tend to before the presentation. Chapter 11 is a checklist of things you might need to bring to your presentation. Chapter 12 addresses the critical importance of practice.

**Part IV, Presenting with confidence**, focuses on the delivery of your presentation. Chapter 13 offers guidelines for facing your audience and making a winning impression. Chapter 14 emphasizes things that annoy an audience and that you'll want to avoid. Chapter 15 guides you in skillfully answering audience questions. Chapter 16 suggests way to manage a challenging audience. Chapter 17 describes techniques that can help you banish extreme nervousness.

**Part V, Tips for selected contexts**, provides guidelines for seven important presentation contexts. Chapters 18 to 24 focus on presenting to management, customers, your team, and foreign audiences, as well as presenting at conferences, presenting webinars, and presenting with co-presenters.

**Final thoughts** concludes the book with some closing reminders.

Throughout this book, I describe many of my own goofs – and successes – and offer the wisdom and experiences of many other people who both give and attend presentations. It is with empathy for the challenges of presenting, and enthusiasm for its joys, that I offer this information.

If you're a nervous novice as I once was, panicked at the very thought of presenting, you'll gain valuable advice, along with my wholehearted support and encouragement. If you already have presentation experience, you'll find numerous tips, guidelines, and recommendations to help you build on your existing skill.

### "But I'm not a performer"

Some technical professionals worry that being a presenter means being a performer. Performers are theatrical. They put on a show. They speak with dramatic flourishes. And that's great – for them. However, you do *not* need to do the same, unless that's what you want to do. Your audiences will respect you if you give an informative, well-delivered presentation.

Furthermore, you can be far from perfect in the mechanics of presenting. A lot of advice available elsewhere on presentation skills is well-intentioned, but overkill for your purposes. Advice such as: hold your hands like this; make gestures like so; stress this word, but not that one; move from this spot on the platform to that spot.

Yes, these things matter, but only up to a point. Most audiences prefer solid content over performance pizzazz. Some of the best presentations I've ever heard were given by people who were clueless about the mechanics, and it showed. But they earned their audience's appreciation by presenting relevant information and ideas in a sincere, engaging, easy-to-grasp way. And that's what matters.

**Introverts and extraverts as presenters**

As an introvert, I want to dispel any notion – especially if you too are an introvert, as so many technical professionals are – that introverts can't succeed as presenters. Introverts are oriented to the inner world of ideas and thoughts. They thrive on quiet and are generally reserved and reflective. They prefer to interact one-on-one or in small groups, and tend to lose energy from interaction. Much more so than extraverts, they process ideas internally before speaking. Many introverts need a lot of quiet time to recharge.

Nevertheless, being more reflective and "in your head" than your more outgoing colleagues need not prevent you from becoming a polished presenter – just the reverse, actually. Introversion can be an asset for a presenter. Although we may be more reluctant to get out there and face an audience, once there, we can excel at presenting.

As my introverted friend Rachel put it, "I'd rather give a presentation to a thousand people than go to a networking meeting." Why? Because for a presentation, she can prepare. She doesn't have to rely on spontaneity and thinking on her feet to succeed. At the presentation, *she* is in charge.

But introverts don't have a monopoly on nervousness about presenting. If you're an extravert, you may be just as uncomfortable about presenting as some of your introverted colleagues. Extraverts get their energy from the external world of people and things. They generally thrive on interaction and gain energy from interacting with others. They tend to be animated and expressive. Much more so than introverts, they enjoy being with lots of people and tend to think out loud.

Despite this "out there" personality, many extraverted people are as reluctant to speak in public as I once was. Nevertheless, if you are an extravert, you can harness that very aspect of your personality to present a strong, compelling presentation.

Indeed, both introverts and extraverts have great strengths as presenters. And both can benefit from coaching, practice, and experience.

### If I can do it

Many prominent speakers began with significant problems to overcome. Winston Churchill had dyslexia, lisped as a child, and stuttered well into adulthood. He had such difficulty communicating that teachers discouraged him from considering a career dealing with the public. A natural orator, he wasn't. Nevertheless, through determination and practice, he went on to become one of the world's most eloquent speakers.

Abraham Lincoln, too, was not a born speaker. Even as president, he wrote down his speeches, and then recopied them and reviewed them until he could repeat them from memory. Although initially ungainly in his demeanor and awkward in his gestures, he overcame these flaws to become an articulate and highly respected orator.

Churchill and Lincoln became skilled presenters. If they could do it (and I could do it) ... so can you.

Let's get started.

# PART I: BECOMING A SKILLED PRESENTER

Imagine yourself giving a presentation that's well beyond whatever you're now capable of. What do you see? What stands out? How do you come across to your audience? By having an image of what you're striving towards, you'll be well on the path to getting there.

This opening section sets the stage for the guidelines and recommendations in this book by providing some tips to help you get started and by helping you appreciate your potential as a presenter.

**Chapter 1, Overview of the basics**, offers some brief guidelines to help you excel at your next presentation.

**Chapter 2, Finding your voice**, challenges you to think big, believe in yourself, and recognize that what you're capable of may be far beyond what you can imagine.

**Chapter 3, Attributes of good and bad presentations**, identifies the attributes that make listeners react positively to some presentations and negatively to others. By reviewing these attributes, you will gain a clear picture of what you should do – or avoid doing – so that the reaction to your presentations is enthusiastically positive.

**Chapter 4, Presentation anxiety and how to tame it**, addresses the fears many presenters have and describes how to start getting them under control. Fortunate are those who have never experienced any presentation anxiety. This chapter is for the rest of us.

# CHAPTER 1: OVERVIEW OF THE BASICS

Your department's work on a complex new system is behind schedule. Your staff, facing last-minute changes and unanticipated bugs, is struggling to keep from falling even further behind. Your customers, concerned about delays, are watching closely. Your CFO is tallying the cost to the company if the release date slips. Your manager keeps asking for updates. The pressure is mounting.

Then who calls but your CIO to tell you he wants you to give a presentation at next week's division meeting? "It only needs to be 20 minutes," he tells you. *Only* 20 minutes!

OK, maybe this situation isn't identical to your own. But if you have a presentation coming up and no time to settle into your easy chair to read an entire book, here are some quick basics for delivering a good presentation:

- Get started.
- Develop the presentation.
- Prepare for the presentation.
- Give the presentation.

## Get started

**First of all, relax**. I know that's not so easy when you're overloaded with priorities. But take a deep breath. Then take a few more. The more clear-headed you are as you prepare for your presentation, the easier the experience will be.

**Identify your biggest fears about presenting**. Then determine what steps you can take to minimize those fears. Make sure those steps include following the guidelines in this chapter.

**Scan the lists in Chapter 3 of the attributes of the best and worst presentations**. Use these lists as a quick reminder of what to do and what not to do in developing and giving your presentation.

You'll find much more on getting started in Chapters 2 to 4.

## Develop the presentation

**Consider your audience**. Who are they and what do they need to know? Tailoring your presentation to that audience will be key to its success.

**Identify the main points you want to make**. Three or four main points are usually plenty for a presentation of up to a half-hour. For a longer presentation, try not to exceed seven main points to avoid overloading your audience. In presenting, less is almost always more.

**Support your main points**. Use such things as examples, stories, statistics, quotes from expert sources, or research findings.

**Plan a strong opening**. It's usually easier to create the opening after you've pinned down your main points. Your opening might include an attention-getter, a statement of objectives, an agenda, an introduction of yourself, an explanation of your handout (if you have one), and any relevant ground rules.

**Plan a strong closing**. Do you want to close with a summary? A recap of key points? A call to action? Think about what you want people to take away.

**Identify how you will involve the audience**. Interaction in the form of discussion, Q&As, exercises, and simulations helps people stay engaged.

**Prepare slides.** Slides aren't mandatory, but if you'll be using them, try to incorporate visuals, such as illustrations, cartoons, clip art, and photos. Minimize the use of bullet points, and strenuously avoid packing slides with text.

**Edit your presentation**. Make changes to improve your material. Delete anything and everything that doesn't support your objectives.

**Prepare supporting material**, if any, such as handouts or notes. Include any detailed information in a handout rather than in your slides.

Much more information on these and related points appears in Chapters 5 to 9.

**Prepare for the presentation**

**Confirm the logistical details**, such as location, date, and the start and end time.

**Review your audio-visual (A/V) requirements**, such as projector, microphone, flipchart, or Internet access. If you'll need A/V support, find out who can help you.

**Identify what you need to bring to your presentation**, such as your laptop, a water bottle, your notes, and a backup of your presentation on a USB flash drive.

**Practice your presentation**, preferably out loud, so you can resolve any flaws and develop fluency in presenting it. Make sure you'll be able to finish by your end time.

**Plan your arrival.** Arrange to be at the presentation venue early so you can address any last-minute details.

Information on all of the above, including a detailed checklist of items that you might need to bring to your presentation, is in Chapters 10 to 12.

**Give the presentation**

**Minimize anxiety** by reminding yourself that most audiences want you to succeed.

**Start strong.** Take some deep breaths, look to the people at the back of the room, and speak directly to them. You will sound confident and that will help you feel confident.

**Know your opening cold.** If it'll help, jot it down on an index card or memorize it (but do not memorize the rest of the presentation).

**Don't disclose any nervousness.** If you feel nervous as you present, don't announce it. Instead, slow down and speak louder. No one need ever know that you're nervous.

**Make occasional eye contact**. Look at people in different parts of the audience. They will experience you as speaking directly to them.

**Use a microphone** to preserve your voice and ensure that everyone can hear you equally.

**Use notes if you need to**, but make sure they are truly notes, not detailed text.

**Monitor your pace**, so that you're speaking at a good pace for easy listening.

**If you make minor mistakes, ignore them**. Stumbling over words or momentarily forgetting what you want to say is normal. Don't call attention to it. Just keep going.

**Avoid annoying your audience**, such as by using irritating mannerisms, speaking too fast, mumbling, reading your presentation, or treating the audience disrespectfully.

**Buy time before responding to questions**. Repeat the question, ask clarifying questions, or solicit input from audience members to gain time to consider your response.

**Answer questions the best you can**, but if you don't know the answer, say so. If appropriate, offer to find the answer and get back to the questioner.

**Handle disagreements**. If you anticipate disagreements, plan your response. Acknowledge the perspective of those who disagree. If they are making a valid point, say so. Always treat audience members with respect.

You'll find detailed information on all these points and many more in Chapters 13 to 17.

**To recap**

Whether your next presentation will be your very first or your next of many, there are some important basics to keep in mind:

- Get started. Try to relax. Think about what will help you avoid your biggest presentation fears. Become familiar with the attributes of the best and worst presentations.
- Develop your presentation. Identify your key points. Add supporting detail and an opening and a closing. Prepare slides and handouts as needed.
- Prepare for your presentation. By taking care of critical logistical details and practicing your presentation, you'll be able to devote your full attention to giving it.
- Give your presentation. Stand tall, convey confidence, connect with your audience, and you'll do a great job.

**In conclusion**

Most audiences prefer solid content to performance pizzazz. I've heard several technical professionals give presentations that fell short in terms of the technicalities of speaking. Nevertheless, they kept their audience's interest because their material was valuable and their delivery engaging.

For much more on the guidelines in this chapter, along with many examples of what works and what doesn't, read on.

# CHAPTER 2: FINDING YOUR VOICE

Geoff, a software engineer in one of my presentation skills workshops, told me during a break that he didn't see how he could ever do what I do. He described himself as reserved and interpersonally clumsy. In his view, my style was animated and enthusiastic and he couldn't imagine himself in those terms.

I could appreciate Geoff's concern; I had the same reaction during my early years as a presenter. I didn't think I could ever excel at public speaking and I certainly couldn't become like some of the highly energetic presenters I'd heard.

Over time, however, I discovered that I could not only become a skilled presenter, but I could do so without changing who I was. In the process, I also learned, to my relief, that there's no need to adopt a style of presenting that doesn't feel right or fit my natural style. The same is true for you. This chapter addresses these points.

## Dare to aim high

I explained to Geoff that my current presentation style differs from what he would have seen if had attended my first several presentations. I pointed out that I'm a different person as a presenter now, and the reason is that I learned how to do what I do. I took classes. I did a lot of practicing. I worked at it. But what helped me develop my skills more than anything else was standing up there, facing the audience, and giving a lot of presentations; gaining experience, in other words.

I reminded Geoff, as I had previously told the class, that like many technical professionals, I'm a strong introvert. But as I gained confidence in my ability to present, I summoned the courage to project more, be more animated, and exhibit a side of myself I never knew I had. "And you can do the same," I told him, "*if* it's something you want to do."

You too are capable of growing as a presenter, and that's the case whether you've yet to give your first presentation or you've been presenting for years. Therefore, don't set arbitrary limits on what you're able to accomplish. Start wherever you are. Build on what you already know and have already done. Then be willing – or have the courage, if that's what it takes – to try new things, including those you never believed possible.

Don't be like my colleague, Emmy, a long-time presenter. As we listened to a speaker demonstrate a storytelling technique, Emmy said, "I don't think I'm ready for this technique yet." To that, I say (and said to her) nonsense! You're ready to try any presentation technique as soon as you decide you're ready.

## Be yourself

One of the biggest challenges in becoming a proficient presenter is finding and refining your style, sometimes referred to as finding your voice. It may take numerous presentations and lots of practice to begin to know yourself as a presenter and to be happy with that person's presentation style. Along the way, you may hear someone speak in a presentation style you admire and find yourself thinking, "That's how I want to present. I want to be just like that person."

I urge caution with that reaction. It's fine to emulate aspects of someone else's style. But *be* just *like* that person? No. Success in presenting means finding your own voice.

If you observe presentation styles that appeal to you, go ahead and see how they work for you. Try them once. Try them a few times. But if they don't feel right, set them aside, because you can't succeed over the long term by being someone you're not. Even in the short term, you'll need to exert a lot of energy to maintain that façade and you'll wear yourself out.

## Believe in yourself

I once coached a project manager, Brian, who had accepted an invitation to speak at a quality assurance meeting. It would be his very first presentation and he was terrified.

When I asked Brian to imagine me as his audience and give his presentation, he stood up rigidly and paused, as if he was trying to remember where he'd stored his voice. When he finally began, his words came out garbled. He started each sentence, then restarted, then started it yet again. He um'd at the beginning of each sentence, at the end, and in the middle. He looked like he was in pain.

After a few minutes, I asked him to sit down and take a deep breath. When he had calmed down, I told him to forget about the presentation and just tell me what his talk was about. In a matter of seconds, he transformed from a panicked presenter into the confident, personable, animated person I knew him to be. In explaining his talk, he effortlessly presented the opening section – the very one he had just garbled – and didn't even realize it.

When I asked what changed when he was seated, he looked puzzled, and then broke out in a big grin as he realized he had just given part of his presentation. Suddenly, he realized he could do it! Sure, he needed pointers (lots) and practice (LOTS). But that's the case for most people.

Believe in yourself. Believe in your ability to learn to give a strong presentation.

## Recognize the imposter syndrome

When I started giving presentations, I saw listeners taking notes. This terrified me. Who was I to be giving advice? Why should they listen to me? What did *I* know?

This reaction, I now know, is called the imposter syndrome. This feeling of inadequacy is familiar not just to technical professionals, but also to many consultants, trainers, speakers, and for that matter, doctors, lawyers, and professors, even when they're doing a great job. So if you experience this syndrome, you're one among many. In fact, if you do a Web search for *imposter syndrome*, you'll find hundreds of links on the subject.

The reality is that when you do a good job of presenting, people listen to you because you have information they can use. You have experience they lack and ideas they can benefit from. You have advice they may find helpful. As you gain confidence as a presenter, you'll stop thinking *Why me?* and instead think, with pride, *Why not me?*

If, moments before the start of a presentation, your inner critic screams, "What are you doing here?" send it out for a snack and get set to give a solid presentation.

## Understand the 3 Ps of presenting

Finding your voice requires preparation, practice, and persistence.

- Preparation ensures you've taken all the necessary steps to do a fine job.
- Practice enables you to feel confident about your material and yourself.
- Persistence helps you gain experience, overcome challenges, and grow as a presenter.

Everything that follows in this book addresses one or more of these three things.

## To recap

If you aim high, believe in yourself, and make a reasonable effort, you can develop strong presentation skills – and without sacrificing your natural style. Whatever your current level of presentation skill, focusing on preparation, practice, and persistence will help you advance. As you do, don't be surprised to see listeners taking notes. Although you may (for a while) see yourself as an imposter, they know better.

## In conclusion

Becoming a confident presenter affects much more than just your ability to present. Many people find that as they develop their presentation prowess, the confidence they gain spills over into their work and personal lives. Conversely, the confidence that develops in these aspects of their lives enhances their competence as a presenter. Don't be surprised if this happens for you.

# CHAPTER 3: ATTRIBUTES OF GOOD AND BAD PRESENTATIONS

You've attended presentations, so you know that some were worth listening to and some wasted your time. Some energized you and some could have cured insomnia. Some capture your attention in the first few minutes. Some, well, you get the picture.

What makes some presentations better than others? This chapter answers this question and helps you determine what you want to do, or avoid doing, in your own presentations.

## An example of a good and bad presentation

Contrast two presenters, Audrey and Bradley. I met Audrey, a consultant to CIOs, when we were guest speakers at an IT off-site meeting. She told me people would be blown away by her presentation and she'd get them thinking in ways they had never considered before.

Instead, she presented in a sluggish manner that sounded more like a lullaby than a wake-up call. She spoke in a monotone, her most critical points indistinguishable from all the rest. Her slides were a jumble of typestyles and clashing colors. She seemed as bored as she was making her audience. Audrey's presentation was a case study in how not to give a presentation.

Bradley, by contrast, is a master presenter who uses stories to make a point or teach a lesson. He laces his stories with details that make the situations he portrays vivid and memorable. He injects humor by finding the humor in everyday experiences. You know from his tone of voice, emphasis, and pauses what's most important.

When Bradley presents, he looks like he's having a good time and is eager for us to have a good time with him. He rarely uses slides. He just talks, very up front and personal. People who have heard Bradley speak once want to hear his presentations again and again.

## The excellent, the mediocre, and the let-me-out-of-here

We know we react differently to different presentations, but what exactly triggers those different reactions? To find out, I posed two questions to colleagues who regularly attend presentations given by technical professionals.

*Think of the worst presentations you have ever heard. What did the presenters do that made them so bad?*

*Then think of the best presentations you have ever heard. What did the presenters do that made them so good?*

If you can resist the temptation to look ahead, spend a few moments thinking about how you would answer these questions.

Here's the feedback I received. See how many responses match your own experiences.

## Attributes of the worst presentations

- Opening with "We have a lot of slides to cover and only an hour to cover them."
- Showing signs of not caring about the audience, the topic, or the presentation.
- Spending too much time establishing their credentials.
- Not explaining what listeners are going to leave with.
- Not stating whether or when questions would be welcome.
- Plodding through half the slides, then racing through the rest, telling listeners they could read them on their own.
- Explaining basic things in a condescending way.
- Providing minimal or no explanation of unfamiliar terminology and acronyms.
- Reading the slides or reading from a script.
- Not engaging the audience.
- Exhibiting tense body language and lack of eye contact.
- Moving around too much.
- Constantly saying um … um … um …
- Lacking spontaneity and speaking in a monotone.
- Facing the screen rather than the audience.
- Belittling people whose views differed from the presenter's.
- Trying to fake an understanding of the technology with technically savvy engineers.
- Dancing around a question instead of admitting to not knowing.

- Showing slides filled with tiny type or difficult-to-read color combinations.
- Having an overload of media: constantly switching among audio, video, slides, etc.
- Being unable to continue the presentation when the laptop died.

How many of these flaws have you observed? Not one of them is trivial; any one of them can lead to a disappointed audience.

## Attributes of the best presentations

- Setting clear expectations about the objectives of the presentation.
- Stating at the outset when it will be all right to ask questions.
- Making eye contact with the audience.
- Using energetic body language and a dynamic speaking style.
- Asking the audience engaging questions.
- Using quick surveys to gauge audience understanding.
- Incorporating an element of mystery or surprise.
- Telling relevant stories.
- Using audio, video clips, or movie clips – in moderation – to balance the use of slides.
- Using diagrams or images rather than bullet points.
- Involving and connecting with the audience.
- Appearing to enjoy giving the presentation.
- Speaking conversationally rather than in a formal tone.
- Establishing a dialogue with the audience.
- Speaking at a pace that's easy to listen to.
- Using humor to connect with the audience.

- Using metaphors and analogies to relate information to everyday things.
- Presenting material that's relevant to today's business environment.
- Using relatively few slides.
- Using slides designed to communicate important and relevant ideas.

I hope you've been able to experience many of these.

What would you add to these two lists from your own experience? Consider using these lists to remind you of what you want to do – or avoid doing – in your own presentations.

To enable you to keep this list handy as you prepare your presentations, I've posted a downloadable copy of it at *www.nkarten.com/PS-BestWorst.doc*.

## Learn from role models

Whether a presentation you attend delights or disappoints you, you can learn from it. Think of the people who deliver these presentations as role models, people from whom you can learn what to do or what *not* to do.

Sometimes, the same person can impress you positively in some ways and negatively in others. For me, one such person was a keynote speaker at an IT conference who failed to consider who his audience was and what mattered to us. He simply gave his pat presentation without making the slightest connection to his audience. His off-putting performance helped me appreciate the importance of learning about your audience and showing an interest in them and their concerns.

At the same time, I was impressed by his ability to speak for an hour without slides, props, or notes. He knew his material thoroughly. That became my goal, to give a keynote presentation without any gadgetry, just the audience and me. Through his inspiration, I achieved this goal much sooner than I might have otherwise.

Who are your presentation role models? Andre Gous, a requirements engineer, offers this suggestion: "As you listen to others, keep notes on how they might have done better or what they did well. Learn from their strengths and weaknesses."

Keep in mind that role models can come from surprising places. One of my favorites is Speakers' Corner in Hyde Park in London. On Sunday mornings, anyone who wants to can stand on a crate or step ladder and speak on any topic at all to whomever gathers around to listen (mostly tourists).

Intriguingly, many of these "presenters" excel at making eye contact, engaging the audience, emphasizing key points, and – since heckling is a both a tradition and an expectation at Speakers' Corner – handling a challenging audience.

**To recap**

This chapter lists many of the attributes that distinguish the best presentations from the worst, as viewed by numerous people who regularly attend presentations. As you prepare your own presentations, scan these lists to remind you what to do or avoid doing. You can add to these lists whatever you've observed from your own experiences as an audience member and from presenters you've identified as role models.

## In conclusion

In presentations you attend from now on, list the things that you find positive or negative about them. Then flag two items on the list of positives that you want to focus on in your own presentations and two items on the list of negatives that you want to guard against. As you master each item, add another one to your list. This is a great way to undertake continuous improvement as a presenter.

# CHAPTER 4: PRESENTATION ANXIETY AND HOW TO TAME IT

Do you ever have dreams about giving a presentation? I don't mean daydreams. I mean dreams at night while you're asleep. I do. In one dream, it was five minutes to my starting time and I couldn't find the room I was to speak in. That, thankfully, has never actually happened. In another dream, it was well after the starting time and I couldn't get the projector to work. Due to the kindness of others, that too has never happened.

There's another dream that still puzzles me. I was giving a presentation on establishing service level agreements and couldn't recall a certain word I wanted to use. While I was struggling to remember it, an audience member asked if the word was "template" – and he was right. How is it that in my own dream, I need help from the audience to remember my material?

Very likely, these dreams are a sign that I feel some anxiety about an upcoming presentation. Indeed, many people feel anxiety while they present or in the days – and in my case, nights – leading up to a presentation. If you experience presentation anxiety, this chapter will help you confront it and reduce it.

## Speak – don't die!

The often-repeated claim is that many people would rather die than speak in public. I'm certain, however, that if any of these people were taken to the edge of a cliff and ordered to speak or jump, they'd make the right choice.

Like phobias, most anxieties are out of proportion to the actual threat. For example, I was amused to read in *Why We Believe in the Unbelievable* by Bruce Hood that although there are no poisonous spiders in the UK, this is one of the most common phobias in the country.

Having looked at photos of poisonous spiders on the Web, I'd say this fear isn't totally irrational. Still, just as with the fear of poisonous spiders in the UK, most presentation anxieties are based on things that aren't likely to occur.

Actually, there are two schools of thought about presentation anxiety. One school says that it's a sign that you haven't prepared. Prepare properly, and you'll be anxiety-free. I know a speaker who is a student of this school and who looks down on anyone who admits to being nervous about presenting.

The other school says that anxiety is common, and as long as you keep it at a manageable level, it's an energizer that will actually make you more dynamic and enthusiastic. That's why it's unwise to use alcohol or drugs to control your nerves.

As you might suspect, I'm a student of the second school. A small amount of presentation anxiety is normal and indeed a plus. Ignore anyone who tells you otherwise.

## Draw comfort from high-level presenters

In fact, despite all the presentation experience they've gained, many people in high-powered positions – CEOs, professors, executive consultants, doctors, and leaders of all kinds – feel some presentation anxiety. For example, I asked a Harvard University professor who frequently speaks to business groups how often he experiences anxiety before presenting. His answer: all the time.

The same is true of professional speakers. When I told my friend, Rob Peck, a long-time professional speaker, how my heart pounded during my very first presentation – the two-minute presentation I described in the Introduction – he said he feels that same pounding even now. Other speaker colleagues have reported the same.

Are these people unprepared? Hardly. The prospect of facing an audience can provoke anxiety in even the best-prepared presenters. Presenting is a form of exposure. You're on stage. You have to fill the allotted time slot. You can't announce, partway through, "That's all I feel like saying right now," and march out of the room. If you experience some presentation anxiety, you're in good company.

Of course, as a master juggler (and a speaker who juggles as he speaks, see *www.zestworks.com*), Rob Peck can't afford to let this pounding affect his performance. But once he starts, he's fine – and so are most presenters. Once we begin, the nervousness transforms into an energizer. So if you experience nervousness, instead of fearing it, welcome it, knowing that your presentation will benefit.

## Identify your fears

Although downhill skiing is nothing like presenting (going downhill when presenting is *not* a good thing), the two are similar in the way anxiety affects them. In his book, *Inner Skiing*, Timothy Gallwey points out that there's magic in skiing when everything is going well. That's also true of presenting.

But in both activities, this magic can turn to misery. When self-defeating thoughts intrude, you lose your rhythm, make mistakes and (at least in skiing), fall and fall again. Anxiety makes you susceptible to fears and doubts, which turn into tension and prevent a skillful performance.

Among the technical professionals I've observed, coached, or interviewed, the most common presentation fears include:

- doing a bad job
- being in the spotlight
- disappointing the audience
- making a fool of yourself in front of peers
- forgetting what you want to say
- coping with things that go wrong
- being criticized by audience members
- having a challenging audience
- responding to questions from the audience.

Which of these do you relate to? What others would you add? Becoming aware of what's *on* your list is a key step in knocking it *off* your list.

## Understand what really matters to the audience

I came to know this list only too well at my very first public presentation, scheduled for the last day of a four-day conference. After three nerve-wracking days, it was finally my turn. Twenty minutes into my presentation, I went blank. I didn't know what I had just said. I didn't know what I wanted to say next. I was mortified. Suddenly, I was facing the first six fears on the list all at one time.

Hours passed. Of course, it was actually just a few seconds, but it *felt* like hours. I found my place, resumed, and ended the presentation more or less upright.

Going blank wasn't a fear I had before this presentation, but it was certainly one I had afterwards.

Still, people seemed to enjoy the presentation. What I eventually learned is that the audience *wants* you to succeed. They'll overlook a lot; they don't expect perfection. Many of them, in fact, are grateful that it's you up there and not them. Accepting these facts shortened my list of fears and I hope it will do the same for you.

Over time, I also learned that even long-time presenters sometimes lose track of what they're saying. To this day, I occasionally go blank. But now, I simply ask the audience what I was saying and they tell me. They don't exclaim, "You idiot!" They *like* being helpful. I've learned that when (not if) I lose my train of thought, I *will* survive.

People expect the presentations they attend to be given by human beings, not robots. Happily, that's an expectation I can meet. And so can you. Therefore, don't become a victim of your anxiety. Instead, be proactive in reducing it to a normal dose of nervousness. Ask yourself:

- What is causing my anxiety?
- What can I do to eliminate it?
- How will I deal with anxiety-provoking situations if (or when) they occur?

### Don't announce your nervousness, minimize it!

Presenters who are nervous are sometimes tempted to tell their audience that they're nervous. That way, they reason, the audience will be forgiving.

Indeed, some audiences *will* be forgiving. Some will give presenters credit for having the courage to present despite their nervousness. When American Supreme Court Justice Sonia Sotomayor's nomination to the Supreme Court was announced on national TV, her first comment was, "I was just counseled not to be nervous. That's almost impossible." I could relate.

Still, think twice about admitting that you're nervous because as soon as you do, listeners will start watching and listening for signs of nervousness – and they'll find signs even if there aren't any. Scratch your nose and they'll see it as evidence of nervousness. Trip over a word, and aha, that's proof of nervousness. Some audience members will focus so intently on detecting signs of nervousness that they won't hear what you're saying.

Instead of announcing your nervousness, take steps to minimize it. These steps will help you sound confident even if you're not.

- Breathe. Nervousness often results in shallow breathing, so take several deep breaths. Deep breathing will slow your heart rate if it's been racing and get you the oxygen that your brain needs to function.

- If you're holding notes, put them down so they don't shake along with you.
- Slow your rate of speaking a bit, speak a little louder, and concentrate on what you're saying.
- Notice negative messages you're giving yourself and focus on positive messages instead. In *What a Great Idea! 2.0*, author Chic Thompson describes this self-talk as giving two presentations at one time, one to your listeners and one to yourself. Young children, he reminds us, don't fall victim to negative self-talk. If they fall as they learn to walk, they laugh, stand up, and try again.
- Follow the suggestions in this book. They will help you feel confident and in control of your presentation and yourself. But if you're overwhelmed by nervousness (or you just like to jump ahead), see Chapter 17 for stress reduction techniques you might find helpful.

**To recap**

Presentation anxiety is common even among some of the most experienced and well-known presenters. Fortunately, a small amount of nervousness is actually a plus: it will energize you and make you a better presenter. To minimize your presentation fears, think about what's contributing to those fears and what, specifically, you can do to eliminate them. Keep in mind that most such fears are about things that won't actually happen. And remember that no one need ever know you're nervous if you don't tell them.

**In conclusion**

Many people want to get rid of their anxiety before they'll consider presenting. But it's by presenting – and gaining experience presenting – that you'll get your anxiety under control. Face your presentation fears and they'll diminish and maybe even disappear.

# PART II: DEVELOPING ENGAGING CONTENT

When you hear presenters who give you the impression that they could speak on any topic at all and make it interesting, what are they doing to convey that impression?

This section identifies key things that make the difference between so-so material and material that will intrigue, inform, and inspire your audiences.

**Chapter 5, Key steps in shaping your presentation**, identifies steps involved in creating a new presentation. The ideas in this chapter will also help you assess your existing presentations to see how you might improve them.

**Chapter 6, Openings and closings**, addresses the two segments of your presentation that frame it and give it structure.

**Chapter 7, Interaction and the adult attention span**, focuses on the use of interaction in making people not just listeners *to* your presentation, but active participants *in* your presentation.

**Chapter 8, The powerful impact of stories**, helps you appreciate your own storytelling ability and includes examples and guidelines to help you incorporate stories into your presentations.

**Chapter 9, Using (without *mis*using) PowerPoint®**, addresses the fact that poorly designed slides are one of the biggest presentation flaws. This chapter guides you in the right direction in your design and use of slides, and in considering alternatives to using slides.

# CHAPTER 5: KEY STEPS IN SHAPING YOUR PRESENTATION

There's no one right way to develop a presentation, but you might find the process easier if you keep in mind the following key steps. As you gain experience, you may prefer to follow a different sequence or to combine certain steps; for example, many presenters edit as they go along, rather than as a distinct step. But this set of steps will help you ensure you haven't overlooked anything critical.

- Get started – now!
- Establish your presentation goals.
- Identify your audience.
- Organize your ideas.
- Incorporate supporting material.
- Accommodate differences in learning style.
- Tailor your material to fit the context.
- Edit your presentation.
- Create slides (if you'll be using slides).
- Take a break.

**Get started – now!**

When will you start developing your next presentation? When you've completed all your other work? The hour before you give it? On the way to the podium?

The correct answer is none of the above. But you knew that, right?

The time to start working on an upcoming presentation is immediately. Your brain is going to start generating ideas for it, so you might as well help it along. When ideas surface, record them. *How* you capture ideas isn't as important as *that* you capture them. At this stage, all ideas are worthwhile. You may end up tossing out many of them, but the ones that remain will be ones you might not have thought of if you waited until you were ready to actively work on the presentation.

**Establish your presentation goals**

Before you do anything else, you need to determine what you're trying to accomplish. Is the purpose of your presentation:

- to educate?
- to inform?
- to persuade?
- to entertain?
- to inspire?
- some combination of these?
- something else altogether?

Now, close your eyes and picture yourself having just finished giving your presentation. You're gathering up your material. You're exchanging pleasantries with audience members. You're grabbing the last crumpet. You're leaving the room. You're done.

As you reflect on the presentation you've just given, answer these questions:

- What were you trying to accomplish?
- What outcome were you seeking? ("Not dying before I finish" is *not* an acceptable answer.)
- How did you want to influence your listeners?

- What did you want them to appreciate, understand, decide, or do as a result of your presentation?
- What reactions did you hope for from them?
- What mood did you want to leave them in?
- What is the most important idea that you want them to remember?

In addition to your goals for the audience, also consider your personal goals. Certainly, you want to do a good job, but what else? For example, do you want to learn more about your presentation topic? Try out some new material? Test the reaction to a new story? Gain experience in answering questions? Remain calm (at least outwardly) while facing a tough audience?

Reflecting on these questions will make your presentation more focused, your message clearer, your points better substantiated, and your delivery more confident. And by articulating your personal goals, you will be more likely to achieve them.

**Identify your audience**

Failure to consider who your audience is can result in a seriously disappointed audience.

I saw an example of this sort of disappointment at an IT division meeting. To broaden the IT personnel's awareness of other disciplines, the CIO had invited a scientist from a local university to speak on nanotechnology research and its medical applications. A fascinating topic! But following an opening that was in our native language of English, he began speaking in the cryptic language of nanospeak, accompanied by incomprehensible slides designed for his academic peers.

This researcher had not considered who his audience was. Granted, he was a busy fellow who didn't have the time to develop a new presentation. But even a small attempt to translate his complex material into everyday English would have enabled his audience to enjoy his presentation instead of being befuddled by it.

Busyness is no excuse. Your presentation is for your audience. If you can't give a presentation that's meaningful *to* them and useful *for* them, you're wasting their time – and your own.

In *Beyond Bullet Points*, author Cliff Atkinson advises that you consider why your topic is important to your audience. How will they benefit from it? What's in it for them? Why should they care? Atkinson suggests that as you develop your presentation, visualize your audience and everything you know about them.

Here are some questions to help you find out about your audience:

- Who is the audience for this presentation?
- What is their background relative to your topic?
- What is their experience and familiarity with the topic?
- What are their needs and expectations regarding this presentation?
- What are their thoughts and feelings about the topic?

- What are some problems or issues they've faced relative to this topic?
- What questions do they have about this topic?
- What kinds of information would they find most helpful?

You might also want to find out if there are terms or topics you should avoid. For example, when an IT manager invited me to give a presentation to his department about managing customer expectations, he stressed that I shouldn't mention service level agreements, a key process for managing expectations. He said his department had been through some serious squabbles over SLAs and if I mentioned them, I'd stir emotions that had finally simmered down. Cut, snip, delete!

Be sure to find out the goals of the person who invited or directed you to give the presentation. If it's your project sponsor or the head of another department, what does the person want the presentation to accomplish? If it's a group from another company, what are their expectations? If it's a special event, what is its theme?

In asking questions, try to learn about the expectations of those who will attend as well as those who invited you. Becky Winant, a software architect, reports that she once mistakenly assumed that the expectations stated by the engineering VP who invited her matched those of the executives who would be attending.

Three minutes into her presentation, she knew it was inappropriate for this audience. The executives needed a simpler, high-level presentation. She talked with the group about their expectations and offered to return two weeks later with a more appropriate presentation. They agreed.

She acknowledges that she might have avoided the false start if she had asked more questions of the VP.

Seek answers to all these questions anywhere you can, including from people in charge of the presentation, people who will attend it, and people in positions or situations similar to those who will be in your audience. As Jutta Eckstein, author of *Agile Software Development in the Large*, points out, these questions determine the types of information and level of detail that will be appropriate for the audience.

**Organize your ideas**

There's no one right way to do this, but a useful starting point is to decide how you'd like to sequence your information, such as chronologically, problem/solution, theory/application, or concept/examples.

Aim to present just a few subtopics within your main topic. Three to five subtopics is usually plenty. More than that and you might overload the audience.

If you compare notes with other presenters, you'll find numerous approaches for generating and organizing ideas. For example:

**Write ideas on index cards**. Write one idea per card, drawing from the ideas you've already captured and adding others as you think of them. Spread the cards out on a table and rearrange them, adding or deleting cards until your material begins to achieve a coherent sequence. Some people write key points on one color index card, stories and examples on another color, and interaction on a third. This visual approach enables you to see if you have a reasonable balance among key points, supporting information, and audience involvement.

**Capture ideas in your presentation software.** I sometimes jot down ideas on slides as raw text and then use the slide sorter to rearrange them. I then add detail to each slide, still as raw text. I don't turn this text into meaningful slides until I've got the presentation mapped out.

**Write a report or an article.** Then convert it to presentation format. Writing helps you develop your ideas more fully. I find that writing an article first helps me generate ideas that I might have overlooked if I focused only on the presentation.

**Create an outline.** As your ideas develop, add detail, such as examples, stories, and so on. Rearrange the outline as you go along.

**Use Mind Mapping® or other diagramming techniques.** With these visual techniques, you start with a central idea in the middle of a page, and then add words, facts, concepts, ideas, and so on in offshoots and branches from the central idea. Do a Web search for *mind mapping* to learn how to do this.

### Incorporate supporting material

Substantiate your information by adding one or two of the following to each key point:

- quotes from relevant authorities
- case studies, examples, or stories
- statistics or research findings
- predictions
- experiences you've had, observed, or learned about

- analogies or metaphors
- activities that will reinforce your points
- illustrations, pictures, diagrams, or models
- anything else that will help substantiate your point.

Move the parts of your presentation around until you've achieved a meaningful flow. Don't be surprised if the sequence of material changes as you refine the presentation. Often, it's not until I'm practicing a presentation that I realize that certain segments are in the wrong place.

When people attend conference presentations, they frequently send tweets (messages of up to 140 characters) to their followers on Twitter, the social-networking site. To make it easy for people to tweet your key points, keep them to Twitter's 140-character limit (or even better, 120 characters so recipients can retweet them, or forward them to their own followers). By the way, reviewing those tweets after your presentation gives you great insight into what audience members considered important.

## Accommodate differences in learning style

People vary in their learning styles. For example, some people are visual learners, some are auditory learners, and some are kinesthetic (or tactile) learners. Visual learners are in the majority, followed by auditory learners. Kinesthetic learners are the fewest. Although most people can learn in all three ways, for each of us, one of these stands out as our preferred method.

Here is what these styles mean in terms of presentations:

- **Visual learners** learn best by observing the presenter's body language and facial expressions, as well as by viewing slides, video clips, handouts, diagrams, props, or other such visually oriented material. Many visual learners would struggle to absorb information that is presented entirely in spoken form.

- **Auditory learners** learn best by taking in information in spoken form, as well as by listening to audio clips, participating in discussions, listening to questions and answers, and interacting with other attendees. Too much emphasis on visual information may cause these people difficulty.

- **Kinesthetic learners** learn best when they can actively participate, taking a hands-on approach. Activities and simulations that give them direct experience with the information presented help them learn. Sitting for extended periods listening and watching may make them restless.

Rather than be concerned about which types of learners you have in your audience, simply assume you have all three and plan your presentation accordingly. For example, a presentation that includes (in addition to your spoken information) Q&A segments, discussion, slides, a video clip, a handout, and some brief activities at intervals will accommodate all three learning styles.

If you're presenting instructions or other information that's critical for people to understand, you'd be wise to present it in both spoken and written form.

To learn more about these styles, do a Web search for *visual auditory kinesthetic learning styles*. In addition, Chapters 7, 8 and 9 focus on how to use interaction, tell stories, and design slides, all things that can help in reaching people with these different learning styles.

**Tailor your material to fit the context**

In particular, consider these issues:

**Audience size:** You don't need to know if it will be 112 people rather than 114; just find out whether it will be closer to 20, 200 or 2000, so you can adjust your presentation accordingly. For example, you might use a more personal style of interaction with a small audience in which everyone can see everyone else than you'd use in a packed auditorium. You might choose to use slides with a large audience, but focus on discussion with a small audience.

Based on Rex Andre's experience, you might want to double check the audience size shortly before the presentation. As a program manager, he was told to expect five to eight managers and technologists at an upcoming presentation. With material for eight people in hand, he arrived to an audience of more than 300! He ably responded by shortening his presentation, identifying key topics, and holding a Q&A session on these topics. Still, it's not the kind of surprise you want too often.

**Timing:** This concerns when the presentation is scheduled during the day or relative to other events or activities. The timing might influence the energy level of the audience and therefore the relative seriousness of your presentation. For example, a presentation at a dinner meeting of a professional association should usually be shorter and lighter than a morning presentation on the very same topic at a technical conference. A presentation after a heavy lunch will need to be lively to keep listeners from drifting to snoozeland.

**Time allotted:** Whether you will have 10 minutes or three hours, the time allotted will influence what and how much you present. If you are an experienced presenter, you know that planning a brief presentation can be more difficult than planning a long one. In a brief presentation, you have to think carefully about what must be included and what can be omitted. For longer presentations, you can take more time to set the stage, tell stories, provide examples, take audience questions, and so on.

One caution: If someone asks you to present in a half-hour what you know requires a half-day, have the courage to say "I can't do that." You will do yourself and your audience a disservice if you attempt to squeeze important material into significantly less time than it requires.

**Breaks:** The advantage of a break during a presentation is that it gives people a time-out from the fatigue of sitting. (As a speaker, I sometimes forget how difficult it is to sit for a long time; when I'm in the audience, I quickly remember.) The disadvantage of a break is that it interferes with the flow of the presentation.

A break is rare in a presentation of up to 60 minutes. Most presenters don't give a break even for 90-minute presentations, although a quick stretch may be appropriate, particularly if people's energy seems to be diminishing.

I usually recommend a break in a two-hour presentation. The biggest challenge occurs with presentations of two-and-a-half to three hours. These time periods are too long for just one break, but too short for two breaks. My preference is to allow a second brief break.

**Type of room:** Will it be an auditorium? A meeting room? A ballroom? The type of room influences how you interact with your audience. But presenter beware: even if you ask, you may face surprises. For an afternoon presentation to a software team, I was told we'd be in a hotel meeting room. I arrived to find that the setting was the ground floor of a beachfront hotel with windows that overlooked the beach. I can compete with other presenters, but bikini babes ...

## Edit your presentation

Carefully limit how much you present. Delete everything that doesn't pertain to your message. Use straightforward language and short sentences. Don't use big words where small ones will do (which is almost always). Edit ruthlessly. You can save what you delete in a "someday" folder.

As Becky Winant notes, "Cramming too much is an error many well-meaning technical people make. Presenting too much information doesn't allow for mental digestion. The audience – who is straining to catch up – hears only your cadence and not your message."

Once, as an inexperienced presenter, I started to develop a 90-minute presentation of three models for managing change. Fortunately, a wise colleague convinced me to take the full 90 minutes to present just one of the models. His guidance saved my presentation.

## Create slides (if you'll be using slides)

Some people advocate staying away from presentation software as you formulate your presentation so you're not tempted to let the slides become the presentation. Other people like to use their presentation software to develop the presentation. My view: try different approaches until you find the ones that work for you.

Just remember, slides should *support* your presentation, not *be* your presentation. You'll find numerous suggestions for creating effective slides in Chapter 9.

## Take a break

Just as audience members benefit from a break during a presentation, you can benefit from one – or several – as you work on the presentation. Periodically get away from it for a few hours or days. When you return to it, new ways of making your points will surface. Things that are out of place will jump out at you. Stories you'd forgotten will reappear. A better arrangement of key points will emerge. You will be bringing new eyes and fresh ideas to the process, and the presentation will improve as a result.

## To recap

In whatever sequence appeals to you, you will find it useful to incorporate the steps in this chapter, such as

- establishing your goals
- identifying the audience
- organizing your ideas
- incorporating supporting material
- accommodating different learning styles
- making adjustments to fit the context
- creating slides
- editing, editing, editing.

As you develop your presentation, give yourself time away from it to allow current ideas to gel and new ideas to emerge.

And, despite how busy you are, start to gather ideas as far ahead of your presentation date as possible. The ideas you collect will help you create a better presentation faster.

**In conclusion**

As you develop your presentations, notice how you go about doing it. You may follow the steps in this chapter or take a different approach. Whatever approach you take may vary over time and with experience. It may also vary with the topic and your experience with the topic. There's no one right way. The best way is the one that works for you.

# CHAPTER 6: OPENINGS AND CLOSINGS

The opening of your presentation prepares people for what they're going to hear. The closing reminds them about what they heard and helps them take away key points. Technical professionals tend to fall short with both of these segments.

In addition to framing your presentation, the opening and closing provide a foundation that supports it. If your presentation is a weekly 10-minute status report to your team, you can skip the formal opening and closing. Otherwise, consider the suggestions in this chapter for delivering a strong opening and closing.

## How to deliver a strong opening

I once attended a presentation for technical support managers given by Tom, an executive from a software company, who opened his talk by saying, "I want to get through the initial slides so we can get to the interesting stuff."

This is no way to open a presentation. If you believe your opening is boring, don't announce that fact to your audience! Even better, prepare an opening that will grab the audience's attention.

The opening is, of course, when listeners form their first impression of the presentation. But don't worry; if you trip over your opening, it's not the end of the world. I've heard both techies and managers fumble the opening and then recover and give effective presentations.

To deliver a strong opening, consider the following six steps, which I describe below:

- Provide an attention-getter.
- Describe your presentation objectives.
- State your credentials (if needed).
- Provide an agenda.
- Explain your handout (if you're providing one).
- Provide any relevant ground rules.

### *Provide an attention-getter*

An attention-getter sets the stage by piquing listeners' curiosity and generating interest in your topic. An attention-getter might be, for example:

- a provocative question
- a surprising or shocking statistic
- a quote from a relevant expert
- a thought-provoking fact
- a relevant story
- a prop that symbolizes your key message
- a comment about the audience or the location.

For example, a presentation to an IT audience on project estimation might open with, "Did you know that more than 50% of IT projects are completed behind schedule or over budget?" Some presenters like to open with a quote from Dilbert, the great master of all things organizational.

I open my managing customer expectations presentations by asking how many people have ever had a negative experience as a customer. Fortunately (for the presentation, at least), almost everyone has had such an experience, and I can use that fact to transition into my talk.

Referring to local events that are meaningful to your audience creates an immediate connection. When I gave a presentation in Germany during the World Cup tournament that Germany hosted, my opening was ready made for me.

As Timothy Koegel, author of *The Exceptional Presenter*, points out, even though it's effective to begin with a statement of your objectives, beginning with an attention-getter is an added plus. Nevertheless, if nervousness is your constant companion, skip the attention-getter and start with a simple statement of objectives, as described next, such as, "Today I'm going to describe three techniques developers can use to ..."

### Describe your presentation objectives

This information sets the stage, letting people know what you aim to accomplish. At events where people have a choice of sessions to attend, your objectives also give them a way to know, right at the outset, whether they want to stay, or attend another session that better fits their needs and interests.

Another benefit of a statement of objectives is that it ensures that you are clear about what you want the presentation to accomplish. If you can't state your objectives simply and clearly, you may need to do some rethinking.

In formulating your objectives, think about what you want people to take away as a result of the presentation. As an example, in my Presentation Skills presentation, my objectives are:

- To help you improve your confidence and competence as a presenter.
- To model some of the guidelines and recommendations I'm presenting.
- To address your presentation questions and concerns.

### State your credentials (if needed)

If everyone in the audience knows you, you can skip this step. Otherwise, summarize your relevant experience. You'll be building credibility with those who don't know you and reminding all the others of your accomplishments. Keep your comments about yourself brief. The presentation may be *by* you, but it's not *about* you.

If someone will be introducing you, note that many introducers don't know how to write an introduction, so it's best to prepare your own. Explain why the topic is important and describe any background that qualifies you to present it. Print your introduction in large type and ask the introducer to read it exactly as it's written.

If it's necessary to remind people to turn off their cell phones (something people should do without being told, but alas, they don't), and you have an introducer, have that person do the "turn off your cell phones" announcement. Doing it yourself will zap a bit of strength from your strong opening.

Look for opportunities to be an introducer. It's a great way to get practice giving a one-minute presentation.

### *Provide an agenda*

I once heard a presentation coach claim that an agenda is unnecessary for a presentation of up to an hour. That's bad advice.

True, some people don't care about the agenda; they're comfortable going wherever a presentation takes them. The rest, however, appreciate structure in their work, in their lives, and in the presentations they attend, and an agenda helps to provide that structure. In addition, it shows that you're taking an orderly approach to your presentation.

You can provide additional structure by referring to your agenda between segments of your presentation. For example, when you finish presenting the first agenda item, you can refer to the agenda again and say, for example, "That covers the importance of developing a testing strategy. Now, let's look at testing techniques that support your strategy."

After one of my presentations, an audience member thanked me and told me my presentation was the only one at the event that began with an agenda. So an added benefit of presenting an agenda is that it distinguishes you from all other presenters who don't do so.

### *Explain your handout (if you're providing one)*

If your presentation includes a handout, it's a good idea to mention it at the outset. Make sure everyone has a copy if it's in paper form. If it's available electronically, let them know where they can access it on their laptop or mobile device.

Also explain whether the handout is a copy of the slides you're showing (as is often the case for presentations by technical professionals) or something else. If it's something else, such as a set of guidelines that relate to the presentation topic, explain whether you'll be referring to it during the presentation or it's intended as supplementary information for later use.

### *Provide any relevant ground rules*

Ground rules for a presentation are simple rules that you provide at the beginning regarding how you'll conduct the session. Ground rules express intentions, alerting people to how you would like to work with them, or in this case, present to them, to prevent circumstances from arising that might cause problems.

One of the most important ground rules (and often the only one that's needed) concerns when and whether you'll respond to questions. If you're willing to take questions (and you almost always should be), responding to them as they arise enables you to address them in context, but requires you to manage your timing carefully. Deferring questions until the end gives you control over your timing, but requires people to delay their questions until long after you've presented the information that generated the question.

A third possibility is to take questions at designated points in your presentation, such as at the end of each subtopic. Whichever approach you prefer, inform people at the outset. Don't leave them wondering whether and when they can ask questions.

Other ground rules might pertain, for example, to:

**Signalling a question**: You might want to let people know that you expect them to raise their hands when they have a question. This might be appropriate if you're speaking to a group known for disruptively shouting out questions.

**Managing time**: For example, "If we're running out of time, would it be all right if I discontinue some discussions in the interest of moving on?" When you frame a ground rule as a question, everyone invariably agrees, thereby giving you permission to do what you stated. I once used this ground rule when I'd been warned that an executive would be attending who had a habit of monopolizing discussions. (Thankfully, he behaved.)

**Giving everyone a chance to speak**: For example: "I'll try to give everyone a chance to comment at least once before giving anyone a second chance." This, like the previous ground rule, is useful in preventing anyone from dominating the discussion.

**Staying on topic**: Require that everyone stick to the topic. This might be useful if audience members might use this gathering to surface other issues that are on their mind.

**Explaining terminology**: Tell people you expect and hope they will let you know if you use a term or concept they don't understand.

## How to deliver a strong closing

A software engineer who gave an articulate, informative presentation betrayed a lack of confidence by ending with,

"I hope this wasn't too boring for you and you're still awake." This is not the way to end a presentation.

Imagine if, instead, he had said, "I enjoyed having you in my audience today. Thank you for attending." He'd have sounded upbeat and confident, and no one would ever know if he felt otherwise.

At another presentation, the speaker abruptly announced, "That's it!" With no warning, he was done. This, too, is not the way to end a presentation.

The closing brings your presentation to an orderly end. It's just as important that you prepare for your closing as for your opening.

In your closing, I suggest that you include these four steps:

- Provide a recap of your key points.
- Invite questions.
- Present your closing comments.
- Thank the audience.

### *Provide a recap of your key points*

It's a good idea to summarize the key points you'd like listeners to remember. You might also display a modified version of the opening agenda slide. For example, in my presentation on managing the chaos of change, my opening agenda looks like this:

- Models that describe the chaos of change.
- A key contributor to the chaos of change.
- Key mistakes in managing change.
- Guidelines for managing in times of change.

With a few tweaks, this same agenda serves as a recap:

- Presented three models that describe the chaos of change.
- Identified a key contributor to the chaos of change.
- Described three key mistakes in managing change.
- Offered nine guidelines for managing in times of change.

### *Invite questions*

If you've taken questions all along and time permits, you can see if there are any remaining questions. If you asked people to hold questions until the end, this is the time to address them.

Either way, pause for a few seconds after inviting questions to allow people to gather their thoughts. Presenters too often ask if there are any questions, and if no one speaks up in the next nanosecond, they resume their patter. Don't do that. Give people a chance to respond.

Alternatively, you can offer your own starting question, such as by saying, "A question that often comes up in this presentation is ..."; and then answering that question. That gives people time to formulate their own questions.

### *Present your closing comments*

When people ask questions at the end of a presentation, others people may tune out or even leave. No doubt, you've been at events at which numerous people headed for the door as soon as the presenter invited final questions. You may even have been one of those people.

To ensure you end your presentation under *your* control and with everyone present and paying attention, try to avoid taking questions as the very last thing you do. Instead, let listeners know that the end of the presentation will take place *after* you've responded to questions. For example: "Let's take some questions and then I'll conclude with three key points I want to be sure you take away with you."

## *Thank the audience*

The audience may signal its appreciation through applause, but whether they do or not, I believe the presenter should thank the audience. And not just a cursory thank you, but a thoughtful one, such as "Thank you for spending this hour with me. I've enjoyed your participation, and I look forward to having you in my audience again."

Of course, if the purpose of your presentation was to inform your staff that their work is being outsourced and they have to train their replacements, you might skip the thank you and run for your life!

## To recap

Haphazardly opening or closing your presentation weakens its impact and effectiveness. As you develop your presentation, think about what you want to include in these segments.

For the opening, consider:

- providing an attention-getter
- stating your objectives
- describing your credentials
- presenting an agenda
- explaining your handout, if you're providing one
- giving instructions for asking questions.

For the closing, consider:

- providing a recap or summary of key points
- taking questions
- presenting your closing comments
- thanking your audience.

You may not need to include all these steps in every presentation, but let your decision to include or exclude them be deliberate. When you frame your presentation with a strong opening and closing, your entire presentation will benefit.

**In conclusion**

As you attend presentations from now on, notice how presenters handle the opening and closing, and think about what you would have done the same or differently if you were the presenter.

# CHAPTER 7: INTERACTION AND THE ADULT ATTENTION SPAN

The adult attention span is short. Very short. Especially among young people.

In the old days, a boring presentation led audience members to twitch, doodle, do crossword puzzles, and whisper among themselves. These days, of course, the distraction of choice is texting, tweeting, Web surfing, and other online addictions, and that's even when the presentation is fascinating. Plan your presentations with this reality in mind.

Some people claim that the average adult attention span is 20 minutes and therefore you'd better say everything important in the first 20 minutes. Others maintain that it's 10 minutes. Do a Web search for *adult attention span* and you'll find claims that vary from mere seconds to 90 minutes!

Obviously, though, our attention spans vary with the situation. I recall a presentation at which my attention span was barely 45 seconds, because I couldn't stand the presenter's arrogant attitude. At another presentation, slide after slide of bullet points caused my eyelids to droop even though the topic was important. But I have fond memories of a 90-minute presentation at which the presenter kept us spellbound. When he finished, we wanted more.

Interaction is one of the best ways to sustain the audience's attention. This chapter offers suggestions for skillfully incorporating interaction into your presentations.

### Types of interaction

Interaction can range from a few seconds to 30 minutes or more. To give you an idea of some of the forms that interaction can take, I'll use my Presentation Skills presentation as an example. This presentation includes the following types of interaction, which I intersperse throughout the presentation.

**A set of "how many of you?" questions.** These questions give me, as well as audience members, a sense of where the audience stands on the subject. For example, to gauge the experience level of the audience, I ask these four questions, one at a time, at the beginning of the presentation:

- How many of you feel nervous at the very thought of giving a presentation?
- How many of you are willing to give presentations but don't enjoy it?
- How many of you enjoy giving presentations?
- How many of you could replace me in giving this presentation?

Having people raise their hands in response to questions you pose is a brief interaction that you can easily incorporate at two or three points in your presentation.

**Laughter.** I include the fourth question: "How many of you could replace me in giving this presentation?" to generate a laugh – an important form of interaction. This question injects a note of levity early in the presentation and communicates that although the topic is serious, we can take a lighthearted approach to looking at it.

**One or more activities.** For example, one of my activities entails having audience members spend a few minutes discussing and comparing their presentation fears with people seated near them. People quickly become engrossed in sharing their experiences. This activity helps them articulate their fears.

**A discussion about the activity.** The discussion following the above activity gives people a chance to describe their own fears and hear each other's fears. This discussion sets the stage for my material on presentation anxieties.

**Stories and examples.** Many of my stories are about my various presentation blunders and what I've learned from them. I also invite audience members to describe their presentation experiences. See Chapter 8 for more on how to use stories to generate interaction.

**Questions from audience members.** I welcome questions throughout this presentation. In addition to my response to each question, audience members often offer their own comments, an excellent form of interaction.

**Q&A.** This refers to question and answer periods at the end of each segment when audience members can ask any remaining questions about the topic we just covered.

**Reverse Q&A.** Here, *I* ask *the audience* questions. For example, when I introduce the topic of interaction, I ask people to identify the instances of interaction I've used so far in the presentation. This question generates interaction about the topic of interaction.

Aim to include some interaction at regular intervals. Doing this will give audience members an energy boost and a respite from listening.

## Other types of interaction

Here are additional types of interaction that can lengthen an audience's attention span:

**Move.** No, I don't mean squiggle and squirm. I mean move periodically from the spot where you're speaking to another spot and speak from there. This minor bit of interaction gives audience members a slight change in their view of you. My colleague, Payson Hall, does a great job of moving through the audience and directing his comments to people seated in various places throughout the room.

**Have audience members move.** For example, partway through my managing change presentation, I ask everyone to move to another seat in the room. We then discuss their reactions to this unanticipated change, which leads to my material on organizational change and how people experience it. Try this kind of interaction if it fits your topic. It's very effective.

**Use props.** My prop collection includes a kaleidoscope that I use to emphasize that people see the same situation differently. Sometimes, I give everyone in the audience their own tiny kaleidoscope, so they can compare what they see. The best props are small, inexpensive gadgets, toys, and everyday items that relate to your message and allow for some interaction.

**Facilitate small-group activities.** Have people divide into small groups in order to solve a problem, review a case study, or discuss an issue. The activity promotes lively interaction among audience members, and subsequent discussion of their findings adds to the interaction. For example, I sometimes ask technical teams to form small groups to identify specific things they can do to better support their internal customers. An activity of even just five minutes is an excellent way to energize people and as a result, extend their attention span.

**Conduct simulations.** My seat-changing activity is a simulation. Another simulation, conducted by Johanna Rothman, author of *Manage Your Project Portfolio*, illustrates the impact of multitasking on productivity and work quality. She has audience members first tear strips of paper from a single sheet, representing a single task, and then alternately from two differently colored sheets, representing two different tasks. This simple, playful activity helps people appreciate that switching between two tasks takes more than twice as long as focusing on just one task at a time, and impairs the quality of the result as well.

## Planning your interaction

Simulations and team activities are among the best forms of interaction. Technical professionals, who by nature like to seek optimal solutions, become competitive, determined to beat the clock, beat the odds, or beat others in the room, adding to the liveliness of the interaction. People can learn more and learn faster from these types of interaction than from a conventional talk-talk-talk presentation.

As valuable as interaction is, don't run an activity just to keep people busy or it will lead them to wonder *What was the point of that?* That was the case, for example, when a presenter asked the audience to participate in a test of their observation skills and then didn't explain how the activity related to the presentation topic.

As you devise various types of interaction, ask yourself:

- What is the purpose of this interaction?
- What is its benefit?
- How does it support my presentation objectives?

As you present, consider adding some interaction (beyond what you already planned) if the audience's attention seems to be dwindling. But be careful about drawing conclusions from facial expressions. Few people grin while listening and a blank stare may indicate blinding boredom – or intense listening. I recall a presentation I gave in which one woman relentlessly stared at me with a glum *I'm trapped* expression. Afterwards, she told me it was the best presentation she had ever attended.

Now, when I see someone staring at me with piercing eyes, I (choose to) conclude the person is exceedingly happy with the presentation.

**To recap**

Sitting still as an audience member was never easy, and these days, with all the distractions we face, it's significantly harder. As a presenter, your job is to keep listeners as engaged as possible. Interaction is a particularly effective way to do this. In addition, interaction can enhance learning in a way that simply speaking to the audience can't.

Consider incorporating interaction at intervals throughout your presentation, such as via:

- discussion
- Q&A
- stories
- individual or small-group activities
- simulations.

Make sure that the types of interaction you select fit your presentation topic and objectives. Notice the types of interaction used when you are in the audience, and learn from them.

**In conclusion**

The more actively involved audience members are in your presentation – participants, in other words, rather than merely listeners – the longer their attention span will be. Keep in mind that people who don't seem fully engaged may have had a poor night's sleep the night before. Their short attention span isn't your fault; they just need a nap.

# CHAPTER 8: THE POWERFUL IMPACT OF STORIES

Here is the gist of a presentation I recently attended:

*Fact, fact, fact.*

*Fact, fact, fact, fact, fact.*

*Fact, fact.*

You could hear the sound of eyelids slamming shut.

For many technical professionals, facts in the form of data, specifications, requirements, code, test plans, bugs, and so on, are where their comfort level is. But in a presentation, facts alone can become boring. Stories that support the facts can enliven a presentation.

According to Chip and Dan Heath, authors of *Made to Stick*, stories are a key element in making ideas and information memorable. This chapter will help you increase your storytelling savvy by focusing on:

- how stories make facts interesting
- why stories work
- where to find stories for your presentations
- stories as interaction
- pointers for storytelling.

## How stories make facts interesting

Consider a story I tell about listening to customers:

Not being listened to is so annoying, as I discovered one evening while at a hotel – and on crutches due to an injury. I suddenly heard the piercing sound of a fire alarm, followed by an announcement that sounded like this: Garble ... static ... crackle ... please use the stairs ... do not use the elevator.

Was there a fire? Or was it a fire drill? Would I have to evacuate in my hobbled condition?

I called guest services. A man answered. I explained, "The announcement was full of static. I'm on the eighth floor and on crutches. I can't use the stairs. Is there a fire?"

His reply: "Please use the stairs. Do not use the elevator."

Talk about listening on automatic pilot! Speaking slowly in hopes of breaking him out of his reverie, I said, "Let me try again ..." Fortunately, this time he heard me. "We'll send someone up to get you," he said. What a relief!

This story underscores several key points, such as:

- Listen carefully when customers speak.
- Don't jump to conclusions about what customers want.
- Confirm your understanding of customers' questions.
- Communicate important messages carefully.
- Make sure your communication systems actually work.

Now, imagine if, instead of telling this story, I simply recited these five points or listed them in a slide? Boring! Whether or not listeners have ever been on crutches on the eighth floor of a hotel when a fire alarm sounded, they've had the experience of saying something important and being ignored or misunderstood. That makes the story universal, a key attribute of presentation stories.

For examples of other stories I use in my presentations, see *www.nkarten.com/PS-Stories.pdf*. Notice how each story draws from an everyday experience to make a point.

## Why stories work

Relevant stories make facts more meaningful. Stories give listeners something they can relate to their own experiences. They have the potential to touch listeners at both a cerebral and an emotional level. They become a springboard for offering recommendations and guidelines. Stories make information easier to absorb and retain. They help you achieve buy-in or acceptance of the points you are trying to convey.

As Garr Reynolds points out in *Presentation Zen*, stories are useful for teaching, sharing, and illuminating.

Stories can be especially important in presentations on technical topics. When I told my seatmate on a recent flight, a professor of cancer medicine, that I was writing this book, he said that the technical presentations his postdoctoral students give are dry and boring, and he's been encouraging them to incorporate stories to add some life – and some human interest – to their presentations.

I subsequently read a book on this very subject: *Don't Be Such a Scientist: Talking Substance in an Age of Style* by Randy Olson. Although Olson's goal is to help scientists communicate more effectively with non-scientists, this book is relevant to everyone who gives presentations.

One of Olson's interesting points is that to reach your audience, first you motivate them and then you educate them. Many scientists, and technical professionals of all kinds, skip the motivation and jump right to the education. What can help motivate them? Stories.

## How to craft a story

Doug Stevenson, author of *Doug Stevenson's Story Theater Method*, advises that in a well-told story, you:

- set the scene
- introduce the characters
- begin the journey
- encounter an obstacle
- overcome the obstacle
- resolve the story.

As he explains, you can then make your point and challenge the audience to accept that point.

Of course, in the technical arena, you don't always succeed in overcoming the obstacle. Sometimes systems fail. Serious bugs emerge. Problems multiply. The usual. In that case, your story might be about the challenges you faced in attempting to overcome the obstacle and the things you tried that you thought would work, but didn't. Then you can advise listeners what to keep in mind if they face similar circumstances.

If you're concerned that you can't tell stories, I assure you that you can, and in fact, often do.

When you vent to your family about the network outage that made you late getting home but that you resolved successfully, you're telling a story.

When you regale your teammates about your customer's meek request for yet another change and how you explained that it'll have to wait until the next release, you're telling a story.

When you tell your friends about completing your project under budget and months ahead of schedule, you're telling a story. (Admittedly, this is a story you may not get to tell very often.)

The main difference between these stories and the ones you tell in presentations is that presentation stories should make a pertinent point that's relevant to your topic. But the story doesn't have to be on the same topic as your presentation as long as the points or lessons that derive from the story are relevant to your topic, as the examples in the next section illustrate.

## Where to find stories for your presentations

One approach to finding stories is to determine the points you want to make and then locate stories to support these points. Another approach, and the one I use, is to notice situations that teach lessons relevant to my presentation topics and make a note of them for future use.

Stories that draw from your own experience are usually the best because you can bring your personal energy and enthusiasm to them. You don't have to memorize the details, because you were there! But you can also tell stories from other contexts, such as history, movies, or books, as well as stories about other people's experiences, preferably with their permission if you'll be using their names.

Whatever you do, don't tell canned stories. These are popular stories that you've heard often – and so has everyone else. And don't tell a story that you heard another presenter tell. That's why your own stories are the best: they're yours, and therefore unique and original.

One of my favorite stories about someone else's experience concerns my friend and colleague, Lou Russell, author of *10 Steps to Successful Project Management*. Just out of the shower one morning at a hotel (not the same hotel as in my crutches story), she turned on the hairdryer and out came … a flame! Fortunately, she hadn't been pointing it at herself. She immediately reported the situation to the front desk and was told, "We don't have any more hairdryers, so you'll have to make do."

What ever happened to "Are you OK?"

I often tell this story to introduce the role of empathy in generating customer satisfaction. Using this story, I don't need to display a slide to make the point. I can just ask the audience: *What was missing in this situation?* (Actually, I sometimes do show a slide, one I created myself that shows a hairdryer with a flame coming out of it. No text, just the image.)

Selena Delesie, a software enthusiast, trainer and coach, tells a wonderful story called "Do You See What I See": *www.selenadelesie.com/2009/02/25/do-you-see-what-i-see/*.

Although it's about nearsightedness, this story is relevant to everyone in the IT and software world, as well as pretty much everyone else. After relating her conversation with co-workers about nearsightedness, she outlines what she learned – and what we can all learn – from the conversation.

But that's not all. She then present several truths, such as not assuming that what you see is what everyone else sees, and describes how these truths are relevant to software testing. The ideas that this story generates could be the basis for an entire presentation. Read it; you'll see.


## Stories as interaction

As I hinted in Chapter 7, storytelling is an excellent vehicle for generating audience interaction during a presentation. Here are some ways to facilitate that interaction:

**Tell a story and ask the audience what lessons they get from it**. Don't be surprised if some of the lessons they cite aren't the ones you had in mind. If your story helps them remember lessons that are important to them, it's as valuable as the lessons you wanted to convey.

**Tell part of a story and ask the audience what they think happened next**. For example, after I describe the guest services chap in my fire alarm story saying, "We'll send someone up to get you," I ask the audience what they think happened next. Some of their guesses are very funny, adding audience-triggered humor to the presentation. I then tell the rest of the story. You'll find the full story at *www.nkarten.com/PS-Crutches.pdf*.

**Have audience members tell their own stories**. For example, I sometimes invite IT professionals to relate memorable experiences they've had as a customer outside of work. People become actively involved in telling their stories and in listening to each other's stories. Their stories set the stage for my material on managing customers' service expectations.

**Ask audience members what lessons their stories offer**. For example, after each story an audience member tells about an experience as a customer, I ask the audience what the experience suggests about the attributes of good service. Their ideas are invariably right on target and provide a perfect transition to a discussion on how they can deliver superior service to their own customers.

### Pointers for storytelling

In telling your stories, keep these points in mind:

**Tell the story first and then draw the lesson**. If you prefer, you can present the lesson and then tell the story, but the story-then-lesson sequence usually has greater impact.

**Keep your stories brief**. Unless you're a master storyteller, a story you tell in several minutes is likely to go over better than one than goes on and on and on.

**Feel free to embellish a bit**. Even with actual experiences, it's all right to tweak a detail or two in order to make your key points. It's a story, after all, not courtroom testimony, and a bit of hyperbole is fine. Just don't mis-state technical details or stray from the essential facts, or you'll lose credibility.

**Engage listeners' senses**. For example, the software engineer in your story has a scruffy beard long enough to sweep the sidewalk. The programmers in your story eat popcorn so buttery you can almost taste it. The company in your story moved to a city so noisy they should have named it Jackhammerville. Rest assured that as you present these descriptions, people will picture the bearded engineer, taste the buttery popcorn, and hear the noisy city.

**Refer to the people in your stories by name**. That way, you avoid repeatedly saying, "The fellow forgot his password … and then the fellow …" Invent names if using their actual names would be awkward for them – or you. Or use humorous names. For example, my husband, who seems to find his way into my stories, has become Mr. Never-Pay-the-Posted-Price and Mr. Honk-If-You-Want-to-See-Aggressive-Driving, among others.

**Vary your pacing and emphasis to fit your story**. For example, speak slowly if you're describing the plodding pace of a customer who keeps fussing over requirements. Pick up the pace if you're describing a deadline that's fast approaching. Slow down again and add emphasis when you're presenting the key takeaway from the story.

**Show, don't tell**. This is sometimes referred to as making the story 3D and is something to work on as your confidence grows. My fire-alarm story is more effective – and more fun to tell – if I hop around the room, as if on crutches, one leg striving not to touch the floor.

## To recap

Some technical professionals naturally incorporate stories into their presentations; for others, the very idea of using stories is unfamiliar. But stories can make a big difference in what listeners hear, learn, retain, and apply.

The best stories for presentations are ones that come from your own experiences and that help you convey key points or teach relevant lessons. You can also use stories to generate audience involvement by inviting listeners to comment on your stories or by sharing their own stories that relate to your topic.

## In conclusion

Because I'm aware of the power of stories in presentations, I see story possibilities everywhere. If you're already a storyteller, you know what I mean. If you're not, I guarantee that once you focus on the potential for the use of stories in your presentations, you too will start to see stories everywhere.

# CHAPTER 9: USING (WITHOUT *MIS*USING) POWERPOINT

Countless books explain how to use Microsoft® PowerPoint® effectively. Trainers teach the topic. Coaches and consultants offer tips. Advice is plentiful.

Nevertheless, most presenters display slides that are cluttered, text-filled, and boring. Worse, they use their slides *as* their presentations rather than to *enhance* their presentations. This problem is particularly common among technical professionals.

Make no mistake: your slides significantly influence your listeners' reaction to your presentation. This chapter will help you make that reaction a positive one.

## PowerPoint: a solution – and a problem

Remember Tom, the high-tech executive in Chapter 6 who began his presentation by saying, "I want to get through the initial slides so we can get to the interesting stuff"? As it turned out, all his slides were crammed with tedious, mind-numbing detail.

The opening of another presentation I heard, this one by an IT manager, featured two slides, each with three multi-line, multi-sentence bullet points. The presenter turned to the screen and read it to us, word for word. Sneaking out began to seem mighty appealing.

PowerPoint is both a solution and a problem. It's a problem because it's so often misused. In fact, a growing number of prominent people have been vehemently discouraging its use.

For example, Edward Tufte, author of numerous books, including the highly regarded *The Visual Display of Quantitative Information*, asserts that the use of PowerPoint is contributing to simplistic thinking and poor decision-making. Furthermore, its use is not to inform the audience but to keep the presenter on course. Tufte is right; too many people use PowerPoint as a crutch.

College students have also been rebelling as more and more lectures are PowerPoint driven. Increasingly, textbooks include slides for each chapter and lecturers who present these slides often sound like they're trying to guess what the slides are intended to convey.

But PowerPoint is also a solution because it offers a visual means of communicating your message, making your spoken information easier to grasp. People who support the use of PowerPoint claim that it's wrong to fault a tool for the way people misuse the tool and that people can learn to use PowerPoint *in service to* the presentation, not *as* the presentation.

Although I fully appreciate the frustrations of those in the first category, I'm in the second category. Since people aren't going to stop using PowerPoint, I prefer to encourage its appropriate use.[1]

## A few simple guidelines for preparing slides

The following six guidelines, which I elaborate on below, can transform slides that are yawn-generating into slides that keep people interested and intrigued:

- Minimize the use of bullet points.
- Present text in small chunks.
- Use a readable type size.
- Limit the use of special effects.
- Use visual images to enliven your slides.
- Let your content determine your slide count.

### *Minimize the use of bullet points*

When people grumble about death by PowerPoint, they usually mean death by bullet points. When slides consist of line after dreary line of text, listeners' brains can't help but shut down as a coping strategy. Nevertheless, many managers require their staff to use bullet points so they can readily review and sign off on the content.

To counter this trend, some people advocate limiting slides to visual images. That's fine for a presentation on your trip to the Galapagos, but for professional or technical presentations, I don't agree. Many people – and I include

---

[1] Everything in this chapter also applies to Keynote®, the presentation software for Apple® computers, and other presentation software. Since PowerPoint is the most widely used presentation software, particularly in the corporate environment, it's the one this chapter focuses on.

myself here – take in information more effectively in text form than via spoken words or visual images. Text used *in moderation* helps us absorb and retain information. Note: *in moderation.*

To make bullet points more palatable, limit the number of words per line and lines per slides. Some people use a rule, such as 5x5: no more than five lines of text per slide and five words per line. That way, each bullet serves as a reminder, enabling you to supply the detail without bogging the slide down with text.

To avoid wordy bullet points, Nancy Duarte, author of *Slide:ology*, recommends that you identify the key words in each bullet point and then delete the rest. This is excellent advice.

Don't worry; if an occasional line has six or seven or even eight words, your audience won't run screaming from the room. But do *not* fill your slides with lengthy sentences.

### Present text in small chunks

People can't simultaneously listen to you and read text-filled slides. Research confirms that we have difficulty processing information that's coming at us in spoken and written form simultaneously. (Do a Web search for *cognitive load theory* for more on this.)

Therefore, if you present text and you don't pause to let people read it, you are forcing them to choose between listening to you and reading the text.

Instead, display each bullet point or chunk of text only when you're ready to talk about it. This is known as *a build*; you're building the content of the slide, one item at a time. You're focusing listeners' attention on that specific item, and they can quickly read it.

Although technical professionals are among the guiltiest of guilty parties when it comes to displaying an overload of text, they are not alone. Even long-time professional speakers make this mistake. Holly, a speaker colleague, showed me the slides for her newest presentation, a well-crafted mélange of images and information. One slide, however, featured four dense paragraphs of text.

I asked Holly if she'd be speaking when she presented this slide. She said yes. When I explained that people couldn't possibly listen to her and read the four paragraphs at the same time, she was surprised. I suggested she divide the information into four slides, one paragraph per slide, and let her audience read each paragraph before speaking.

In considering what she was attempting to convey, she realized she didn't need all four paragraphs to make her point. She deleted three of them.

Once you start to think about these guidelines, you too will start to see the flaws in other people's slides.

### *Use a readable type size*

I recall a presentation by an IT consultant whose slides were filled with text the size of ants. Fortunately, we had a handout of his slides. *Un*fortunately, even at only two slides per page, the text was unreadable.

That situation struck me as a good gauge: if you can't read the text on a slide at a two-slides-per-page size, it's too small. Usually, 24 points is a good size for easy reading, with headers and titles at 36 points.

Most important, discard all slides that lead you to say, "I know you can't see this ..." Or, as one presenter at a software testing conference said as she displayed a flowchart filled with impossible-to-see text, "What's in these boxes isn't important." If your audience can't see it or it's not important, omit it!

Keep in mind that older audiences have poorer eyesight than younger ones. Before my presentations, I often ask people in the front row why they chose to sit there. The most common answer is that they want to be able to see the slides. This is a statement about the prevalence of unreadable slides in presentations they've attended.

### *Limit the use of special effects*

Video clips, audio clips, sound effects, and music are excellent ways to add variety to your slides, but if you use too much of any of these, or switch frequently among them, listeners will become annoyed.

Also, strenuously resist the urge to use every fancy option – spinning text, snazzy transitions, repeated dissolves, and so on – unless they support a point you're making. Even then, don't overdo it. What seems clever if you use it once or twice can become tiresome by the third time and downright irritating by the fourth.

Be especially careful about using color combinations in your slides that look enticing on your computer screen, but that blur your message when viewed on a presentation screen. When I see slides with yellow text on an aqua background or blue text on a black background, I know the presenter hasn't looked at the slides from the audience's perspective.

## *Use visual images to enliven your presentations*

Visual images, such as drawings, cartoons, photos, charts, illustrations, and video clips, can help you make your points in a more dramatic fashion than text alone. For example, when you tell a story, display a visual that captures the essence of the story. A single image, especially one that's unexpected or amusing, can convey your point, while letting the audience listen to you rather than read bullet points.

Consider an example provided by Garr Reynolds, author of *Presentation Zen*, regarding the level of air pollution in a particular city. His advice: display some dead birds or a diseased lung. The emotional impact of visuals, such as these, will make it much more likely the audience will absorb and retain your message.

A project manager in one of my workshops complained that she couldn't use visuals because she wasn't creative. Not so, I told her. She simply hadn't gained experience in locating, selecting, and using visuals. What she needed wasn't creativity, but rather an awareness of the possibilities.

For example, you don't have to look at more than a few slides created by Kim Laursen, an IT education coordinator (*www.nkarten.com/PS-KimSlides.pdf*), to grasp that photos can provide a background for your text. She designed her presentation around the theme of an adventure and located photos to support that theme. Even bullet points are easier to take when displayed against a captivating, colorful background.

Or take a look at a few of the many slides created by Ellen Gottesdiener, a consultant and author of *Requirements by*

*Collaboration* (*www.nkarten.com/PS-EllenSlides.pdf*), and you'll see how you can use downloadable photos or create your own sketches to help you make your point.

Finally, a few slides from one of my own presentations show how I use whimsical cartoons (*www.nkarten.com/PS-NaomiSlides.pdf*) custom-drawn for me by Mark Tatro, a superb illustrator (*www.rotategraphics.com*). These clever cartoons add a light touch, enabling me to use minimal text and making the task of creating slides fun.

Where do you find visuals for your slides? Here are several possibilities:

- Interesting or unusual photos you take yourself. Most likely, you have a camera handy. Start using it to take photos for your presentations. Or review the photos you took on your vacation.
- Websites, such as *www.iStockphoto.com*, that offer photos, illustrations, and video images at little or no charge. Do a Web search for *low-cost images* for other sources.
- Websites, such as *www.animationfactory.com*, that offer animated clipart, templates, and video.
- Clipart. Do a Web search for *clip art CDs* and *royalty-free clip art*. The possibilities for customizing clip art to make it fit your presentation are endless.
- Drawings that you create freehand, or by using sketching tools, such as *www.sketch.odopod.com* (this is fun!).
- Drawings made for you by art students who are eager for the experience and will charge little or nothing.
- In-house staff who can assist you in preparing your slides.
- Kids or friends who are artistically talented.
- Professional illustrators, such as Mark Tatro.

- Video clips that you create yourself or find online. (I've been told that using video clips from YouTube and other public access sites does not violate copyright. However, I've yet to hear this from legal authorities and would urge caution.)

Some people have told me they don't have time to search for visuals, and I certainly understand. At the same time, other equally busy people have told me that finding suitable visuals is easy. In fact, PowerPoint itself offers visuals in the form of clip art, word art, symbols, photos, and more. But if you don't have time to locate visuals for your next presentation, then just be alert for any you might like to use at some future time.

Of course, if you're giving a one-time-only presentation and time is limited, visuals may be the easiest thing to omit. Just make sure you don't overload your listeners with border to border text.

### *Let your content determine your slide count*

Some coaches recommend 10 slides as the maximum for a presentation. Others say 25. In my view, advocating a specific number misses the point. Ten slides might be too few if they omit critical information that people can't grasp strictly from listening.

At the other extreme, 75 slides might seem excessive for a one-hour presentation. But I attended a presentation in which every one of the 75 slides was a photograph of an amusing scene or sign that supported the speaker's points. The speaker brilliantly synchronized his slides with his patter, resulting in a first-rate presentation.

Sometimes more slides are better than fewer. For example, in my Presentation Skills presentation, I discuss nine points on presentation delivery. Instead of squeezing all nine points into a single slide, I divide them into four cartoon-enhanced slides: *www.nkarten.com/PS-FourSlides.pdf*. The result is slides that are easy to read and fun to look at.

The question is not *How many slides do I need?*, but rather *How can I design slides that will enhance my presentation?*. From that question, the right number of slides evolves.

**Supplement your presentations with handouts**

When people talk about handouts in conjunction with a presentation, what they're usually referring to is a display of the slides used in the presentation. Organizers of many conferences expect presenters to submit their slides in this format to be printed for attendees or posted online for downloading.

On the one hand, handouts that display slide images save listeners from having to take notes about the slide contents, enabling them to focus on listening. On the other hand, slide-oriented handouts give listeners no detail beyond what's in the slides.

If you'd like to provide a handout that includes additional information, you have many choices. For example:

- Provide a handout that maps to the slides, but for each slide includes additional information in a text format.
- Include supplementary information in the handout, such as relevant articles or related guidelines.

- Include links in the handout that listeners can use to access related articles and information.

An important use for a handout that technical professionals often overlook is to present information that displays poorly on the screen (the "if you can't see this" types of information). For example, if you need to display tiny text, such as to explain a coding technique, provide the code in a handout. You can then use a laser pointer to point to the code in your slide and the audience can follow along in their handout.

In general, use a handout to present data, charts, lists, or anything else that's difficult to read on the screen. If your slides look like a report, move the detail into a handout and use the slides to sum up the report. Or give out the report and skip the slides. Indeed, some executives encourage their staff to write a report first and then create a presentation that highlights the key points.

Preparing a handout is an added task, but it keeps people from having to squint and enables them to concentrate on the presentation. Plus, a handout gives people something to take away that includes your contact information so they know where to reach you.

**Seek alternatives to slide-driven presentations**

What are your options if you want to use few or no slides? In addition to using handouts, you can use interaction, team activities, simulations, stories, and notes posted on flipcharts.

Another approach is to make the entire presentation a discussion. After a discussion-oriented presentation on

*Resistance as a Resource* by Dale Emery, a consultant and expert on this topic, numerous attendees thanked him for not using slides. Using examples that he solicited from the audience, he discussed their challenges, asked thought-provoking questions, and helped them see the options available to them.

But just in case an audience balks at the absence of slides, Dale has his full set of slides ready to use. For people who want something tangible to take away, he also provides the full set of slides for the event proceedings.

To use this approach successfully, you need to know your topic well and, like Dale Emery, be a master empathizer who excels at engaging an audience. A discussion-oriented session can be an energizer for both the audience and the presenter. When you feel ready, give it a try.


**Additional resources**

For additional inspiration, and a bit of amusement, here are some links you may find useful:

- Any of the presentations at *www.TED.com*, such as:
  - *www.ted.com/talks/lang/eng/joshua_klein_on_the_int elligence_of_crows.html*
  - *www.ted.com/index.php/talks/hans_rosling_shows_th e_best_stats_you_ve_ever_seen.html*
  - *www.ted.com/talks/dan_pink_on_motivation.html*
  - *www.ted.com/talks/beau_lotto_optical_illusions_sho w_how_we_see.html*
- How (Not) to Present with PowerPoint (Don McMillan, video – this one is very funny!): *www.presentation-*

*skills.biz/%20presentation-delivery/how-not-to-present-with-powerpoint.htm*
- New evidence that bullet-points don't work (Olivia Mitchell): *www.speakingaboutpresenting.com/design/%20new-evidence-bullet-points/*
- Is PowerPoint Dumbing Down Our Decisions? (Joe McKendrick): *www.smartplanet.com/business/blog/business-brains/is-powerpoint-dumbing-down-our-decisions/1709/*
- Top Ten Slide Tips (Garr Reynolds): *www.garrreynolds.com/Presentation/slides.html*
- The problem with PowerPoint (BBC News Magazine): *http:/news.bbc.co.uk/2/hi/8207849.stm.*

Do a Web search for *PowerPoint presentations* for many others.


**To recap**

Many people badly misuse presentation software, forcing audiences to suffer through their presentations. To avoid falling into this trap (or to escape from the trap if you're already in it):

- Minimize the use of bullet points.
- Present text in small chunks.
- Use a readable type size.
- Limit the use of special effects.
- Use visual images, preferably lots of them.
- Let your content determine your slide count.
- Use handouts, where feasible.

And remain open to the possibility of eliminating slides altogether and using discussion, simulations, and other types of interaction instead.

## In conclusion

If you choose to use slides, do so thoughtfully. As you create each slide, consider how it will help or hinder the success of your presentation. Imagine how you would react if you were an audience member viewing the slide. If you're going to continue to use presentation software – and let's face it, most of us are – remember: *you* are the presenter; let your slides support you, not replace you.

# PART III: PREPARING TO PRESENT

Benjamin Franklin said, "By failing to prepare, you are preparing to fail."

Still, how nice it would be if all you had to do after you developed your presentation is show up and give it. That may be possible if you regularly speak to the same group. For all other presentations, this section will help you remember key things you might otherwise overlook

**Chapter 10, Logistical preparations**, describes important details that can make or break the best-developed presentation. By paying attention to these details *before* you show up to present, you'll have several fewer things to worry about *when* you show up to present.

**Chapter 11, Presenter survival kit**, offers a checklist of things you may want to take to your presentation. Some of these things are so obvious that you'd never forget them (or would you?). Some are things you may not realize you need until you need them. This checklist will help you remember more of what you shouldn't forget.

**Chapter 12, The vital role of practice**, addresses why practicing your presentations is so important and offers some ways to do so. If you're a new presenter, practice is critical. But even if you're a highly experienced speaker, you need to practice if you want to continue to impress your audiences.

# CHAPTER 10: LOGISTICAL PREPARATIONS

Failure to pay attention to the logistical preparations outlined in this chapter can ruin a presentation. Let the following suggestions guide you in addressing logistical details that are part of every successful presentation:

- Dress to unstress.
- Review your audio-visual requirements.
- Confirm the location and date.
- Meet your deadlines.
- Be on site well ahead of time.
- Be prepared to end on time.
- Take care of yourself before your presentation.
- Determine what you need to bring with you.

## Dress to unstress

In many companies, casual attire is the norm for technical professionals, unless they will be seeing customers in which case more business-like attire may be required. But what's permitted on the job may not be appropriate when you're giving a presentation.

Generally, it's advisable to dress so that you look similar to your audience, or at least not too dissimilar. A business suit would be out of place in a casual-Friday meeting, but might be appropriate at a CEO meeting (unless, of course, it's held at a golf course). Shorts and a t-shirt won't make you popular at a formal awards ceremony, but might be just right at a conference for developers at a fun-in-the-sun location.

If you don't know what kind of attire is appropriate, ask the person who invited you. Once you know, review what you'll wear. That way, you won't run the risk of discovering at the last minute that the shirt or blouse you had planned to wear has a splotch of mustard from last week's dinner meeting. Oops.

Don't wear anything you haven't tested for comfort. It's hard to maintain your composure when your new shoes are strangling your feet. If you'll be traveling to give your presentation and ink stains are attracted to you, a backup outfit might be a good idea.

**Review your audio-visual requirements**

Will you be using slides? If so, who will arrange for the projector? Do you know how to connect your laptop to the projector? If not, who will assist you, or who can help you learn to do it yourself?

Will you need an extension cord? A microphone? A laser pointer? A wireless remote for advancing your slides? A flipchart and markers? An Internet hookup? Is a wireless connection available? Who will ensure that the A/V equipment is in working order before you show up?

Look into these issues well ahead of your presentation; otherwise, they can become serious distractions and major sources of stress.

If you'll be displaying slides, note that projectors vary and incompatibilities sometimes occur between the projector and the laptop. Many companies have A/V staff or a designated person who can help you get your equipment set up and running. Most conference centers and hotels also have staff that can assist. Find out ahead of time who can help you if you run into a problem.

## Confirm the location and date

If you're unfamiliar with the location, please, please, don't make assumptions. A few years ago, I was invited to speak to a technical group in Bad Homburg, Germany. I assumed that Bad Homburg was the German way of saying Hamburg. Just before making a flight reservation, I looked up the city on the Web. Oh nooo ... The town of Bad Homburg is 500 km away from the city of Hamburg. Yet another lesson learned.

I learned a related lesson when my faraway friend, Judith Marx Golub, offered to drive me to my presentation at a convention center near her home. Which she did. Only one problem. It was the wrong convention center. The right one, we discovered, was several towns away, but where, exactly, she wasn't sure.

Fortunately for me (and her), we made it with entire minutes to spare. We now laugh about the experience. And I now make sure I can provide the precise location to those I'm depending on to get me there.

Also make sure you know the presentation date. Make *very sure*. As program director for his Project Management Institute chapter, Neil Lapham, a Senior Project Manager, awaited the arrival of a speaker, Alex, at a monthly meeting. Time passed. No Alex. Finally, Neil called him, fully expecting to hear that he was simply delayed in traffic.

When Alex answered in his usual upbeat voice, Neil was shocked to discover that Alex thought the presentation was the next week. It turned out that Alex had had a computer crash and didn't realize until that very moment that when he restored everything, some dates had become distorted.

This is a harrowing experience for anyone in charge of arranging a presentation, especially if they have to scramble to find a replacement. It's also mortifying for the presenter, especially one who, like Alex, takes his commitments seriously. So check and double check your own schedule. And don't depend on your technology to remind you when to show up.

**Meet your deadlines**

The people who coordinate conferences and meetings typically notify presenters of due dates for such things as submitting a presentation abstract and identifying audio-visual needs. When presenters miss their deadlines, these coordinators can't meet their own deadlines. Meeting your due dates is a little thing with a big impact.

Granted, meeting these deadlines can be a nuisance, and it's not, as if you've got nothing else to do. But because it's so common for people to miss their presentation deadlines, you'll make a positive impression by delivering on time. Or deliver early and build a reputation as a reliable and trustworthy presenter.

**Be on site well ahead of time**

A half-hour ahead might be sufficient, but I suggest at least an hour if it will be your first time at this venue. Allow enough time to take care of any problems. Caution: just like software bugs, some presentation problems take longer to resolve than you would like.

Jude Rajan, a software engineer, would agree. As design lead for a project, he was presenting to a cross-functional group that included business partners. He arrived 15 minutes early, which was normally enough time. What he found in the room, though, was a jumbled mass of network cords. With the audience seated and watching, he needed 20 minutes to untangle the mess and get the one cord he could use. Situations like this lie in wait to prevent an unruffled on-time start to your presentation.

And truly, there's no end to surprises. In visiting a company for a speaking engagement, I arrived an hour early. When I checked in at the security office, I was told I would have to watch a security video and pass a test before I'd be admitted onto the campus. It's always something.

## Be prepared to end on time

If your start time is delayed, it's still your responsibility to end on time. That means you may need to condense your material or present only a portion of it.

Fortunately, such situations are rare. If you're concerned, create a shorter version of your presentation as a backup. Or do as Malcolm Kushner, author of *Presentations for Dummies*, suggests and organize your material into modules, each of which addresses a specific subtopic. That way, you can select a set of modules to fit the time available.

Whatever you do, don't do what a presenter named Gary did. In the best of cases, Gary seemed to be competing in the high-speed presentation Olympics. When the schedule slipped and he had a mere 20 minutes instead of an hour, he did the impossible. He spoke even faster. To make matters worse, Gary's slides were packed with bullet points – and he seemed determined to address every bullet point in every slide. By his sixth slide, my ears begged for mercy.

Be kind to your audiences; be prepared to speak at a reasonable pace *and* end on time.

**Take care of yourself before your presentation**

My colleague, Francesco Ientile, a sales specialist, emphasizes that just as professional athletes warm up so as to perform at peak levels, you need to start your presentation warm. If you're going to speak with energy and enthusiasm, you need to be in a state of energy and enthusiasm before you start. Decide in advance what you need to do to get into that state.

In addition, get enough sleep. Eat right. Warm up your vocal cords by finding a quiet place before your presentation and talking to yourself, singing, reading, or whatever you choose so your voice is ready to go.

And this may not need saying, but don't forget a toilet break before your presentation, especially if you're nervous about presenting. When I solicited advice from speaker colleagues, several mentioned this point. It's difficult to speak calmly when you feel the urge to be elsewhere.

## Determine what you need to bring with you

Despite having an IT background (or perhaps because of it), I'm paranoid about things going wrong. Therefore, I always bring a copy of my slides on a USB flash drive in case I need to switch to another laptop.

But a backup won't help you if you don't know where you put it. That's what I learned the time my screen went blank partway through a presentation. Up from the audience popped my colleague and friend, Andre Gous, to give me his laptop.

Great, I thought, I'll just get my flash drive. But where had I put it? In my computer case? But which pocket? Or had I moved it elsewhere?

Lesson #1: If you bring something with you that you might need urgently, make sure you know where you put it.

Fortunately, Andre quickly discovered that I didn't have a laptop problem. I had a vision problem! The outlet I had plugged my laptop into was in a hard-to-see spot and I hadn't fully inserted the plug into the outlet. The laptop had been running off the battery, which had run down. Andre plugged it in properly and it sprang back to life. Happy ending. Thank you, Andre! Thank you, thank you!

Lesson #2: Make sure what you plug in is *really* plugged in.

Lesson #3: Bring a small flashlight to your presentations.

What else do you need to bring with you? See the next chapter for a detailed list.

## To recap

It's not enough to create a great presentation. Before you're ready to give it, you have to tend to logistical details that can make the difference between success and humiliation, if not outright failure. This chapter reminds you to:

- dress appropriately
- anticipate your A/V needs
- confirm the presentation location and date
- submit required information in advance
- arrive on site early
- prepare to end on time
- stay in good physical condition
- bring a backup copy of your presentation.

## In conclusion

As you develop your presentation, think about what you need to do to prepare to present it. Create a list so that you don't forget anything critical. Draw from past experiences. The better you take care of the logistical preparations, the more relaxed you'll be at show time.

# CHAPTER 11: PRESENTER SURVIVAL KIT

Here is a list to use as a reminder, so you don't forget anything you need to bring to your presentation. You may not need all these things, but it's better to have them and not need them than need them and not have them.

- **Your laptop.** This may seem too obvious to put on a list, but if you're list-oriented, include it. Don't forget the power cord. Make sure your slides are loaded on your computer if you'll be showing slides. And don't leave your computer at security at the airport. Amazingly, people do this all the time.
- **An extension cord.** Some meeting rooms are not designed for meetings! If there are audio-visual staff on site, they can usually supply an extension cord if you need one. But you might want to bring your own just in case.
- **A network cord.** This will come in handy if you'll be going online and you're presenting in a place that doesn't have a wireless connection.
- **Electrical accessories.** For presentations outside your country, determine if you'll need plug adapters, power converters, or other electrical items. If you're not sure, do a Web search for *electrical requirements for [country]*.
- **A wireless remote.** This device enables you to advance your slides from a distance, so that you don't need to be standing at your laptop keyboard as you present. Most remotes include a laser pointer.
- **A USB flash drive with a copy of your slides.** If your laptop misbehaves and you have to use someone else's, a

backup copy of your slides will be a life saver. You may also want to upload your slides to a website. That way, if your slides get clobbered and your flash drive refuses to cooperate, you can download the slides.

- **A printout of your slides.** I'll never forget the meeting director who sheepishly told me that he'd brought the screen to the meeting but forgot the projector! Using my printout as a guide, I was able to deliver the presentation. The meeting director was beyond grateful.
- **Presentation notes.** You might do just fine without notes. But if you positively need them, it might be worth bringing two copies, just in case one disappears en route.
- **Your handouts.** If you're providing a handout, there may be a meeting organizer who is in charge of reproducing it and having it on site for you. It's a good idea to check with this person in advance to ensure the material will be on site as planned. Bring a master copy that you can use to make copies, just in case.
- **Any relevant supplementary material.** This may include, for example, books you want to display or quote from, props you use in your presentation, and material that you want to hand out after the presentation.
- **A small flashlight.** This can come in handy in many ways, such as for seeing the connectors on your laptop or on the audiovisual equipment. A small hand mirror can also be helpful in seeing connectors that are nearly inaccessible.
- **A pocket knife.** This is valuable if you'll be opening taped boxes in which you shipped your materials. If you're flying to a speaking destination, be sure to pack it in your checked luggage, not in your carry-on bags.

- **Paperclips**. In addition to their obvious uses, paperclips can fill in as a pocket knife in opening packages if you don't have a knife with you.
- **Flipchart**. Usually, flipcharts are available at meeting venues, so submit a request if you'll need one or more. Before you start, make sure the flipchart has enough paper. Otherwise, you may discover 10 minutes into your presentation that there are only two sheets left and you've already used one of them.
- **Flipchart markers**. Often, the markers provided with flipcharts are worn down or are in colors that are impossible to see from a distance. Bring your own so you have the colors you prefer and you know they'll work.
- **A timer**. Don't depend on your watch to keep track of time; repeatedly glancing at your watch suggests you're unsure of your timing – or you can't wait until you're done (which may be true, but if so, don't let it be obvious). I use a small travel alarm clock that I can see from a distance
- **A notebook or pad**. This will be handy for ideas you want to record before or after your presentation (or during).
- **A pad of sticky notes**. These are handy for jotting down quick reminders. I write my ending time in red on a sticky note that I place near the projector, because once I start speaking, I sometimes forget what time I'm supposed to end.
- **Several pens**. Why, I don't know, but, people often attend presentations without a pen. Before my presentations begin, someone often asks me if I have a pen they can use. My answer is always yes.

- **Tape**. Bring whatever kind you'll need. For example, you might want masking tape if you'll be posting flipchart sheets on the wall. Special types of masking tape are available that won't leave a mark when removed.
- **A recording device**, if you'll want to record your presentation. You'll find it valuable to listen to your recordings afterwards to learn what you did well and what needs work.
- **Your cell phone** if you might want to call someone during your presentation. Yes, I've seen presenters do this, though only for humorous purposes. *Make sure* you turn it off before you start presenting.
- **A camera** if you might want to take a photo or a video of the audience. If you're going to take audience photos, ask for their permission first – and always obtain permission before you post photos online.
- **Business cards** to give audience members or people you meet. If your company doesn't provide business cards, do a Web search for *free business cards*, or design and print your own.
- **A snack**. A growling stomach is not a melodious sound effect. If your flight – or your previous meeting – runs late, a snack will prevent you from starving before (and while) you speak.

- **Lotion and hand sanitizer**. The lotion will help protect you from winter dryness if you're in a cold climate. The sanitizer will help protect you from people with germs.

- **Water.** Speaking generates thirst, and speaking while thirsty is uncomfortable. Meeting rooms often have water available, but don't count on it. Bring your own.
- **Backup eyeglasses.** This may be overkill. But if you're someone to whom things happen, such as taking your glasses off and sitting on them, a backup pair might be wise. Don't forget reading glasses if you need them.
- **Tissues.** Don't let that unexpected sneeze catch you unprepared. Achoo!

**To recap**

Before you head to your presentation, use this list to ensure that when you arrive, so will everything you need to have with you. Don't forget to ask yourself:

- What would I add to this list?
- What have I forgotten in the past that I wish I had remembered?
- What have I previously had handy that I never imagined I'd need?

**In conclusion**

I've used this list several times since I created it for this book. I can't believe I didn't create it years ago!

For a copy of this list in Word format (without my added comments), see *www.nkarten.com/PS-SurvivalKit.doc*. You can rearrange or modify the list as you choose for your own presentations.

# CHAPTER 12: THE VITAL ROLE OF PRACTICE

When you don't practice your presentation, it's obvious to listeners that they *and* you are hearing it for the first time. Although practicing is the one of the most important contributors to a successful presentation, it's one that busy people often skip. This chapter explains why and how to practice.

## Why practice?

Practicing helps you look, feel and sound professional and prepared. Consider these benefits:

- You can't be certain you know your material until you try it out loud. Furthermore, as software architect, Becky Winant, points out, once you speak the words aloud, you may have a little less trepidation about speaking them for the first time "live."
- Practice helps you present a strong opening. In fact, you might practice your opening more than the rest, since that's when you're most likely to feel nervous.
- Practice makes you sound more conversational, rather than stiff and formal.
- You can make sure you have your *um's* and *ya'know's* under control.
- Words, phrases, or ideas that make sense when you think about them might come out garbled when you attempt to speak them. Practice helps you recognize when you need to find a better way to make your point.
- If you'll be using slides or other audiovisuals, you'll get better at synchronizing them with your speaking.

- If you'll be conducting a demo, you'll become smoother at coordinating the demonstration with your speaking.
- If you'll be using notes, you'll get better at referring to them without interrupting your flow. You may soon find that you don't need your notes.
- If you need to read your presentation, you'll become more familiar with your material and more skilled at maintaining eye contact with the audience as you read.
- You'll confirm that you have the right amount of material for the time allotted, and the right amount of time for the material you've prepared.
- You'll be able to gauge your timing to be sure you'll end on time.
- You'll become able to present the key points without reading your slides.
- You'll remember additional details, examples, stories, and key points that you want to incorporate.

- You'll notice changes you want to make, as well as material you want to rearrange or delete.
- You'll discover whether any parts of the presentation seem dry and need attention.
- You'll determine whether you've adequately balanced facts with stories, examples, and interaction.
- You'll be able to tell your stories more effectively. Nothing ruins a story more than, "Wait, I forgot to mention the …"

# 12: The Vital Role of Practice

## How to practice

Practice any way you can. Work on individual parts until you feel comfortable presenting them. Record your presentation and listen to it. Present all or part of it for colleagues and get their feedback. Practice in the shower (if it's a short presentation or a long shower).

An excellent way to practice is to join Toastmasters (*www.toastmasters.org/*), a wonderful organization with clubs all over the world that hold one-hour meetings weekly to help people improve their presentation skills. Some companies sponsor their own Toastmasters club. The meetings provide a safe setting in which to practice presenting and get caring feedback. Some clubs videotape presentations so members can see what they're doing well and what needs improvement. I've met numerous technical professionals who participate in Toastmasters and rave about the experience

Or work on your presentation privately (as I do). First, run through it silently until you get the biggest bugs out. Then speak it out loud, start to finish, in a quiet place where you won't be interrupted. Notice where you run into problems or stumble over words. Make adjustments right then and there or note what needs attention and come back to it later. Spend extra time on any parts that give you trouble. If you feel excessive anxiety as you practice, it may be a clue you need more practice. Or it may be that you need to practice techniques designed to reduce anxiety, such as those in Chapter 17.

**To recap**

Don't overlook the critical importance of practicing your presentation, especially if you are a nervous novice. This chapter outlines the reasons to practice. Whether you practice by yourself or in a setting in which you can get feedback, you'll be transforming what might otherwise be a mumbling, bumbling, stumbling presentation into one you'll be proud of.

**In conclusion**

As you develop experience, you may be able to limit your practicing to the parts of your presentation that are new or revised. But don't rush it. As Eric Bloom, president of Manager Mechanics LLC, notes, it's better to be over prepared than under prepared. Practice your presentation until you *really* know it. Then you can skillfully handle whatever transpires.

# PART IV: PRESENTING WITH CONFIDENCE

This section addresses issues that significantly influence the successful delivery of your presentation.

**Chapter 13, How to make a winning impression**, describes things to keep in mind as you face your audience. Whatever your current level of presentation experience, take a close look at this chapter.

**Chapter 14, How not to annoy your audience**, acknowledges that we all do things unintentionally that can irritate an audience. By identifying the most common annoyances, this chapter helps you avoid them. One less thing to worry about.

**Chapter 15, How to handle audience questions**, offers tips on how to respond to audience questions when you know the answer and also when you don't.

**Chapter 16, How to manage a difficult audience**, addresses that dreaded situation: an audience that gives you a hard time. If you worry about having a difficult audience – or even just a difficult audience member – this chapter offers suggestions for handling the situation.

**Chapter 17, How to conquer nervousness**, recognizes that even if you follow all the advice in this book, you may still feel a distressing level of nervousness. This chapter describes techniques that can help you reduce that nervousness to a manageable level.

# CHAPTER 13: HOW TO MAKE A WINNING IMPRESSION

It's time to face your audience. This chapter offers 11 recommendations for making a positive impression and avoiding mistakes that many technical professionals make:

- Build rapport with the audience.
- Open with confidence.
- Speak in your own natural voice.
- Make eye contact – and you contact.
- Don't become dependent on your notes.
- Use a microphone.
- Present standing.
- Avoid the need to read.
- Monitor your pace.
- Use humor judiciously.
- Observe your presentation as you give it.

## Build rapport with the audience

Building rapport is about starting before you start. The 10 or 15 minutes before you begin your presentation is a chance to mingle with audience members, chat with them, and win some supporters – unless you're presenting bad news, in which case it may be wiser to stay out of sight until it's time to start.

I acknowledge that mingling is not for everyone, sometimes including me. Mingling entails making small talk, and that's something many introverts (and some extraverts) don't enjoy doing. But sometimes it's worth pushing through any discomfort you feel in order to connect with your audience. Greet as many people as you can. Ask about their challenges regarding the presentation topic. Find out what questions they have.

People are usually flattered to be asked and pleased that the presenter is interested in them. As requirements engineer, Andre Gous, points out, you'll then have a few islands of friendly people in your audience.

## Open with confidence

Since your opening will strongly influence your audience's perception of your presentation skills, it's important to project an air of confidence when you begin. Therefore, you might want to take a few moments before starting to be alone and center yourself.

When it's time to begin, take your place, pause for a few seconds, and take a deep breath. Smile at the audience – or at least try not to look unhappy (even if you are). Then look at a specific person and speak to that person, as if you're having a private conversation. Or look at a person in the back of the room and speak to that person. Starting this way will make you look and sound confident, and that in turn will make you feel confident.

If you're nervous about presenting, the opening is when you're likely to be most nervous. If that's the case, try memorizing your opening lines or jot them on an index card in case you need them.

## Speak in your own natural voice

Something about standing in front of an audience makes some people abandon their everyday natural way of talking and instead sound stiff and formal. People will find it easier to listen to you and will be more receptive to your message if you speak in a down-to-earth, conversational manner, pretty much the way you normally speak.

Except for any relevant technical terminology, use familiar, everyday language. If you use pretentious, multi-syllabic words, you'll sound like you're talking down to your audience. And avoid long, complex sentences. I excel at speaking in sentences that are so long and convoluted that halfway through, I'm as confused as the audience, so this advice is for me as well as you. Remember, if you confuse your audience, you lose your audience

## Make eye contact – and you contact

I recall a software designer who stared at the floor as he spoke, as if he believed that if he couldn't see us, we wouldn't be able to see him. Some presenters do something similar, looking anywhere as they speak but at the audience. Others look at the audience, but their eyes dart so rapidly from one audience member to another, it's a wonder they don't get dizzy and topple over.

The issue is simple: you can't connect with your audience if you don't look at them. Yet, making eye contact is one of the most difficult things for inexperienced presenters to do, and it's no less difficult for many experienced presenters. There's something intimidating about looking someone in the eye while you're speaking.

To make it easier, think of eye contact as *you* contact: presenting so that you make contact with several different audience members. Look at one person as you present some ideas or a few points. Then look at another and do the same. Speak to each, as if that is the only person you're speaking to. They will experience you as speaking directly to them, which is exactly what you're doing.

## Don't become dependent on your notes

If you use notes, make sure they're nothing more than an outline, a few reminders, or something specific, such as a quote that you want to be sure to state accurately. Detailed notes will entice you to keep peeking at them to make sure you didn't omit anything, giving the audience the impression that you don't know your material. You will also be tempted to read your notes, rather than speak naturally.

If you prefer to use notes, plan ahead. Will you use full-size pages or index cards? Will you hold your notes or have them nearby for occasional reference? Will you need to turn pages? Whatever your choice, practice so you can handle your notes smoothly.

Don't let notes become a crutch, as I did for too long. I was afraid to present without having my notes handy. Then one day, I was scheduled to speak in an ultra-hot-weather location. As soon as I reached the convention center, I realized I had left my notes in my hotel room, two hot, sweaty blocks away. I couldn't bring myself to go back for them. Forced by meteorological conditions, I gave my presentation without my notes and discovered I didn't need them.

If you use notes for fear of forgetting something, keep this in mind: your audience doesn't know your presentation. If you omit a point, they won't know. If you forget to tell a story, they won't know. If you remember a point you meant to mention earlier, simply mention it now. They'll never know.

## Use a microphone

For most presentations, it's wise to request a microphone. Otherwise, if you speak loudly enough to be heard in the back, you'll be shouting at the people up front. Conversely, if you speak at a comfortable volume for those up front, the people in the back won't hear you clearly. A microphone enables all listeners to hear you equally.

Furthermore, a microphone preserves your voice. I learned this the hard way the time I forgot to ask for a microphone. Twenty minutes into my presentation, it started to rain. And thunder. And hail and howl. We were in a one-story building that felt the full brunt of the storm. Foolishly, I tried to outshout the storm. I succeeded – and spent the rest of the week with a raspy voice and sore throat.

If you're not familiar with microphones, try to arrange a practice session. A handheld microphone can feel awkward at first. If you're using a lapel microphone, people may not be able to hear you if you turn your head away from it. Little details like these make a difference.

Whatever you do, do *not* start your presentation by tapping on the microphone and asking, "Can you hear me?" Check out all your equipment *before* you start.

## Present standing

When you stand while presenting, you're more energetic, forceful, and persuasive than if you're sitting. You can move around at will, gesture readily, and breathe more easily. You appear confident even if you don't *feel* confident.

Some presenters are most comfortable standing behind a lectern[2]. That's understandable; a lectern confers a feeling of safety. Unfortunately, few technical professionals are skilled at sounding spontaneous and energetic when using a lectern. Therefore, I encourage you to avoid the lectern and face your audience front and center.

Alternatively, give part of your presentation from behind the lectern and part out front. The one time I used a lectern was my first keynote, for an audience of 2,000. I wasn't using slides, and I feared venturing too far from my notes. But whenever I told a story, I moved to the center of the stage. Try this approach if you use a lectern and want to wean yourself away it.

In certain situations, sitting while presenting is preferable to standing, especially if the group is small and you want a setting that's conducive to discussion. In such situations, I try to arrange for the group to sit in a circle so everyone can

---

[2] A lectern is the piece of furniture that holds a microphone and provides a place for your notes — not to be confused with a podium, which is a raised platform that you stand on.

see everyone else. And of course, speak while seated if you have a physical constraint that keeps you from standing. Audiences are sympathetic to genuine constraints; there's no need to prove anything.

## Avoid the need to read

I'll never forget a software manager named Vince who read his presentation, word by dreary, monotonic word. In short order, several people tiptoed out. Then a few more left and a few more until the room was half empty. An optimist might say it was half full, but when half the once-occupied chairs become vacant, I assure you the room is half empty.

Thankfully, Vince finished 20 minutes early. Amazingly, despite having driven away half his audience, he asked if anyone had questions. Someone asked a question and he answered adroitly. More questions followed; he responded skillfully. Clearly, he was capable of speaking fluently and energetically.

As Vince demonstrated, when you read your presentation, it's difficult to sound spontaneous or convey enthusiasm. Furthermore, people who read their presentations often lose their place, such as the director of global communication technology I heard who read the same line three times before he realized it. If you have to read your presentation, practice reading it so that you know your material and you don't have to gaze continuously at your text.

Reading slides to the audience is a related problem. Technical professionals who read their slides convey a lack of confidence. As Tobias Fors, a software development consultant, comments, "Listening to someone reading slides makes me think the person doesn't know the topic very well." As he points out, when a presenter is confident, it's easier to believe what the person is saying.

## Monitor your pace

If you speak at a slow, plodding pace, people will fall asleep, read their e-mail, or tiptoe out (the tiptoeing is to avoid waking those who remain behind). If you speak too quickly, they may stay if you're presenting important information, but your pace will frustrate them.

Nevertheless, when some people present, they speak faster or slower than they do either in an everyday conversation or when practicing their presentation. To avoid falling into this trap, simply notice your pace as you present, varying it as you naturally would in speaking to another person. Ask yourself periodically if you need to pick up the pace or slow it down.

Monitoring your pace also means keeping track of your timing. As you practice, note where you are at various points, such as at 15-minute intervals or at the end of each key point. Then when you're presenting, notice where you are at these time markers. If you've fallen behind, you can speed up a little so you finish on time. If you're ahead, you can expand on subsequent points (or finish early, which no one will complain about). But be careful – if you're far ahead of where you should be, you may have been speaking too fast and need to slow down.

One other important aspect of monitoring your pace relates to pauses. Allowing a few moments of silence makes some presenters feel uncomfortable, as if they have an obligation to fill every second with patter. But pausing actually gives people time to absorb your information.

Therefore, pause when you finish presenting a key point. Pause before saying something that might be a surprise, such as the end of a story. If you're showing slides, pause before advancing to the next slide. Pause when you invite questions.

If I were stating the last four sentences in a presentation, I would pause for a few seconds after each of them.


**Use humor judiciously**

Humor is appropriate in most presentations, but make sure your humor has a point that's relevant to your presentation. And don't make the audience the butt of your humor or you risk embarrassing or annoying them. Instead, aim for humor that pokes fun at yourself. But just a little; too much self-deprecating humor ceases to be humorous.

Avoid jokes unless you're a natural joke-teller and are confident you won't garble the joke – or the punch line. The last thing the audience needs to hear is, "Oh, I forgot to mention the part where ..." If you're determined to tell jokes, practice them until you've got them perfect.

Humor usually works best after the audience has listened for a while and become familiar with your style, so use caution in opening with humor unless you're known for it and skillful at it. Stay away from the usual controversial topics: politics, religion, and so on. What's funny to you may offend listeners.

Actually, some of the best humor occurs when an audience member says something that everyone finds hilarious. You can't plan for it, but when it happens, it's often funnier than anything you'd have come up with yourself. And if you're lucky, you'll occasionally say something spontaneously that amuses the audience. If the audience laughs at your unplanned humor, enjoy the moment and laugh with them. Afterwards, make a note of what was so funny. Who knows? Maybe there's a way you can work it in next time around.

## Observe your presentation as you give it

Perhaps you've had the experience of trance driving: you drive someplace and when you get there, you have no memory of actually driving there. A similar phenomenon can occur when you present. To avoid trance presenting, reserve a portion of your awareness to observe yourself, your audience, and the environment.

I came to appreciate the importance of this observation when I gave a presentation at a summertime technical training conference. Afterwards, an audience member commented, "Too bad the air conditioning was turned up so high. I was freezing." Others had similar comments.

Strange. I was warm enough. How could *they* have been freezing?

Then I realized: as I presented, I was gesticulating and moving around, generating body heat, and oblivious to my teeth-chattering audience. When people are freezing, they shiver. They scrunch up to conserve warmth. They put on sweaters. If I'd stayed alert, I would have noticed people attempting to cope with the frosty conditions.

At the other end of the thermometer, I once gave a presentation in a room that was so hot that people used my handout as a fan! I stayed in denial and continued, as if everything was fine. The miracle was that no one walked out.

What I should have done in both situations is to notice the uncomfortable situation, empathize with the audience, and determine if I (or someone) could address the situation. If you do as I should have done, at least the audience will know you're aware of the situation even if you can't fix it.

I heard an excellent example of addressing the situation in a stifling hotel ballroom. A few minutes into her presentation, the speaker said, "This room is uncomfortable. Would someone find a person who can turn on the ventilation?" And someone did. Clearly, it's permissible to acknowledge a problem and seek help in resolving it. In fact, people admire you all the more when you do.

In observing your presentation as you give it, ask yourself:

- How are people responding? Do they seem to be with me? Do they look restless? Is it time for an energizer?
- How is my pace? Should I speed up? Should I slow down? Should I vary my pace more?
- Is my volume appropriate? Should I vary it?
- Am I pausing enough to let people absorb my message?
- How is my timing? Should I expand on the next point? Should I abbreviate some points to ensure I finish on time?

## To recap

The recommendations in this chapter address matters that can make a significant difference in the audience's reaction. So remember to:

- Connect with your audience.
- Open strong.
- Speak in your natural voice.

- Make eye contact.
- Preserve your voice by using a microphone.
- Present standing, preferably front and center, rather than from behind a lectern.
- Speak spontaneously; don't read your presentation.
- Keep track of your pace.
- Use humor if you want to, but do so carefully.
- Focus a tiny bit of your attention in observing your presentation as you give it.

Rest assured, as you become increasingly experienced, every one of these things will become natural.

**In conclusion**

If you keep these recommendations in mind, you'll do a fine job in delivering your presentation – provided, of course, that you don't annoy your audience. That's the topic of the next chapter.

# CHAPTER 14: HOW NOT TO ANNOY YOUR AUDIENCE

This chapter describes an assortment of things that might annoy an audience:

- physical mannerisms
- vocal mannerisms
- clichés
- speaking too fast
- excessive apologies
- treating the audience with disrespect
- tentativeness
- mumbling.

Many of the technical professionals I've coached have been guilty of one or more of these things. So have I. That's because they are all things we might say or do during a presentation without even realizing it.

The starting point in eliminating possible annoyances is to become aware of them. That's what this chapter will help you do.

## Physical mannerisms

We all have mannerisms, things we say or do that are harmless but that might annoy an audience. For example, some people sway as they speak, as if they're on a boat being rocked by the waves. I was in the audience for one such presentation, and after a while, I felt like we were all swaying side to side along with the presenter. It's not often that an audience becomes seasick while listening!

Of course, the problem with a mannerism like this one is that we may not know we're doing it until someone gives us feedback (hopefully gently).

Other physical mannerisms include twisting your hair, rubbing your hands together, twirling a pencil, gesticulating wildly, as if you're on fire, pushing your glasses up, scratching your nose, tap-tap-tapping on a table, jiggling coins in your pocket, pacing, and chewing gum. Yes, chewing gum! IT education coordinator Kim Laursen told me about a gum-chewing presenter she heard. If any of these mannerisms are things that you do, be mindful of their potential as annoyances and strive to eliminate them.

Some presentation coaches suggest that you practice your presentation in front of a mirror to identify your own potentially annoying mannerisms. It's worth a try, but seeing yourself in a mirror is so unlike giving an actual presentation that you may not behave as you would in front of an audience. Far better is to be filmed speaking so you can see what you're doing that you might be unaware of. Or get feedback from a coach or from colleagues at an actual presentation.

**Vocal mannerisms**

A presenter named Max, OK? had the bad habit, OK? of interspersing every few words with an irrelevant word, OK?

until after a while all I heard, OK? was his repeated OKs, OK? Max was the head of a successful software development company and a technical genius, but would you have enjoyed listening to him for an hour?

*OK*, as Max used it, is a pause filler, a pattern of speech that includes such favorites as *ya'know* and the ever popular *um* and its cousin *uh*. Those who study such things (yes, *um* is the subject of research) point out that pause fillers exist in every language.

In the book *Um: Slips, Stumbles, and Verbal Blunders, and What they Mean*, author Michael Erard describes research that shows we each having our own pattern of um frequency and usage. Some people *um* within a sentence, some *um* between sentences, some *um* a little, some a lot, some not at all.

Complex sentences sometimes result in um-filled pauses as you figure out what you're going to say next. If that's your experience, use short sentences and slow down so you can think ahead. Whatever you do, *don't* let *um* be the first word of your presentation.

Certainly, if you use pause fillers frequently, you'll sound unprepared and unprofessional. But don't go crazy trying to avoid them. Pause fillers are part of everyday conversation and they sometimes seep into a presentation. Just keep them to a minimum. Actually, some storytelling groups view an occasional *um* as making a story sound spontaneous rather than carefully rehearsed.

## Clichés

Clichés, of course, are phrases that are overused, such as:

- old as dirt
- big as life
- cute as a button
- to go through the roof
- at the end of the day
- the low-hanging fruit
- like shooting fish in a barrel
- busier than a one-armed paper-hanger.

Some clichés are universal; others are location-specific. If you use an occasional cliché, don't worry; hardly anyone will notice. But a cliché-riddled presentation will peg you as unoriginal and uncreative. Seek imaginative way to make your points. Can you come up with three original variations of *old as dirt*?

If you do a Web search for *clichés*, you'll find numerous websites that offer lists of clichés. If you're unsure if a phrase you want to use is a cliché, check out these websites. Of course, if you're giving a presentation on the use of clichés, these websites are a goldmine (to use a cliché).

**Speaking too fast**

Speaking just a little fast isn't a serious problem. But *too* fast is a major annoyance.

I recall one such presenter whose speaking speed made my brain hurt. During the break, the meeting sponsor asked him to slow down. When he resumed, he joked about his rapid pace and said he'd speak more slowly. And he did. For about three minutes. Then he raced through the rest of his presentation. He had excellent material and a seriously disappointed audience.

Why do some people turn speaking into a speedathon? It might be due to the fear of not getting through all the material in the time allotted – or having too much material for the time allotted. Or it might be due to nervousness and the subconscious thought that "the faster I speak, the sooner I can get out of here." For some people, though, it's just a bad habit.

If you're a speedy speaker, imagine that you're presenting to people who aren't fluent in English. Pause periodically, especially after you've made a key point, to give listeners a chance to absorb your information. Get feedback from colleagues or a coach, and if they tell you you're speaking too fast, try to s-l-o-w down.

## Excessive apologies

Alfred, a disaster recovery specialist whose luggage had gone astray en route to the event, opened his presentation by apologizing for his inappropriate attire. As he spoke, he apologized again and again. The first apology let the audience know that he knew he wasn't in professional garb. After that, his apologies became annoying.

Clearly, Alfred's plight was uncomfortable for him. But to the audience, there was no plight. He was the victim of circumstances over which he had no control and everyone could relate. By repeatedly calling attention to the situation, he risked ruining an otherwise good presentation.

If you face a situation in which circumstances are other than you would have liked, mention it once, apologize and provide an explanation if appropriate, and then proceed. Don't belabor the point.

**Treating the audience disrespectfully**

Magicians have a saying, "If your act is mediocre and they love you, you are a good magician. If your act is fabulous and the audience doesn't care about you, you are a poor magician." I learned about this saying from Payson Hall, a consulting project manager and an amateur magician who enjoys baffling me with his magic tricks.

Payson once attended the performance of a world-famous magician who forgot his responsibility to his audience. The magician's performance was flawless. But when his attempt at involving the audience in a particular trick didn't go as he had planned, he became mean, impatient, and arrogant. In so doing, he lost the affection of the audience. His extraordinary skill no longer mattered.

The same is true in presenting. If you offend the audience or treat them unkindly, a flawless presentation won't keep them from dismissing you as a failure.

Even something as simple as using acronyms without explaining them might feel to the audience like a sign of disrespect, particularly since some acronyms have multiple meanings. Sherry Heinze, a test consultant who often attends presentations, points out, "I have the most trouble when the acronym is familiar to me, and my familiar acronym stands for something entirely different from the speaker's."

Clearly, succeeding as a presenter requires attention both to *what* you present and *how* you present it.

## Tentativeness

Tentativeness refers to softening your word usage so much that you sound like you lack the confidence to say what you believe. A common example of presentation tentativeness is frequently prefacing opinions and recommendations with *I think*, such as "I think project managers should ..."

Another sign of tentativeness is saying *a bit* or *sort of* or *kind of*, as in "His report was a bit lacking in details." These weasel words reduce the impact of the statement. As a stronger alternative, try "His report lacked certain key details."

Don't worry; no one will notice an occasional *I think*. And it's sometimes appropriate to soften your advice, such as by saying, "You might want to consider ..." That way, it's clear you're offering a suggestion and not issuing orders. Just try not to sound as if you're afraid to state your views.

## Mumbling

Might listeners hear *sit* when you say *set*? Or *50 percent* when you say *15 percent*?

I attended a presentation by a business analyst who was puzzled when we reacted negatively to her description of a colleague as an apathetic person. It took several minutes of debugging for us to figure out she was actually describing the colleague as an *empathetic* person. If listeners seem confused by what you've said or ask you to repeat what you said, they may be offering you a mumble alert.

To find out if you mumble, record your presentations and have someone else listen to them and give you feedback. Notice when other people muffle words in presentations, conversations, or phone messages, and make a point of not doing the same. For an example of a muffled phone message, see my article, *For a Good Time, Call 333-3333* (*www.nkarten.com/PS-333.pdf*).

Be particularly careful with words that people often get lazy about in everyday conversation:

- Say *to*, pronounced like *two*, not *tuh*.
- Say *want to*, not *wanna*.
- Say *going to*, not *gonna*.
- Say *doing*, not *doin'* (enunciate those final g's).
- Say *you*, not *ya* (as in *ya know*).

Do a Web search for *enunciation exercises* for websites that provide phrases and tongue twisters for practicing your enunciation.

**To recap**

Being human means occasionally saying or doing things in a presentation that might annoy audience members. Most annoyances are things we can easily avoid once we become aware of them, such as:

- physical mannerisms: using distracting gestures
- vocal mannerisms: frequently using *um* and other pause fillers
- clichés: relying on overused words and phrases
- speaking too fast: rushing so that people can't absorb your information
- excessive apologies: repeatedly apologizing when just once is sufficient
- treating the audience with disrespect: offending the audience

- tentativeness: sounding like you lack confidence in your own views
- mumbling: speaking as if your hand is covering your mouth.

By becoming aware of your own annoying habits, whether these or any others, you can purge them from your presentation repertoire.

## In conclusion

Whenever you hear a presenter whose mannerisms or speaking style annoy you, think about whether you ever do the same. If you do, take steps to avoid a recurrence. Sometimes, something as simple as a sticky note with a big red "slow down" or "enunciate" reminder is all you need. *Voilà*, problem solved!

# CHAPTER 15: HOW TO HANDLE AUDIENCE QUESTIONS

Many technical professionals have told me that one of their biggest presentation fears is being unable to answer questions from the audience. Trepidation about questions is understandable. It's the fear of standing there like a goofball saying, "Duh, uh, mmm, well, let's see …" and hoping that someone sets off the fire alarm so that you'll have to leave the building, at which point you can escape. This chapter will help you successfully respond to questions.

## Facing audience questions

If you fear audience questions, I relate to you. As a novice presenter, I used to plan my presentations to end precisely at the ending time so there would be no time for questions. I was certain I'd be unable to answer them. People would catch me not knowing. I'd be mortified.

Then one day, I gave a presentation that changed my perspective. When I finished, the moderator said, "We have some time. Would you like to take some questions?" Noooo, absolutely not! That's what I thought, but of course, I had no choice. I said I'd be happy to.

Someone asked a question. I answered it. Someone else asked a question. Again, I knew the answer. Another question and another. My responses felt ragged and jagged, but at least I had something to say. How about that? I can answer questions! And so can you.

## Preparing to answer questions

The starting point in responding to questions is to think about who will be in your audience and what questions they might ask. Have colleagues help you come up with questions. Formulate responses to these questions and practice presenting them so that you can do so articulately if they come up during the presentation.

I sometimes tell my audience right at the beginning that I hope they'll ask at least a few questions that I can't answer since those questions will give me something to learn. Then, if such questions arise, I thank the questioners for doing what I'd hoped – and I seek help from the audience in responding.

If you'll be presenting to a small group, try to talk with group members individually beforehand, in person if possible. Talking with them may give you insight into what they might ask – and make them less likely to ask tough questions. This kind of preparation is especially important if you'll be presenting to a demanding audience, such as a board of directors or customers worried about another slipped deadline.

Use the reciprocity principle to your advantage. That is, people tend to want to do a favor for those who have done them a favor. If you do something helpful for these individuals before your presentation, they may return the favor by going easy on you. Still, your ability to withstand a barrage of tough questions could be a career-enhancing opportunity.

**Responding when you're unsure of the answer**

Inevitably, questions will come up for which you don't have a ready answer. This can pose a particular problem for introverts, because many of us introverts can respond more articulately if we can ponder the question for a while before responding. Alas, in a presentation, you can't just stand there pondering. Still, whatever your personality, you can buy time by trying the following:

**Repeat the question**. In addition to ensuring that everyone has heard it clearly, repeating the question gives you a few seconds to contemplate what you want to say – and you can do a lot of contemplating in those few seconds. Even as you're repeating the question, your mind is at work coming up with a response.

**Clarify your understanding**. After you've repeated the question, you can gain a few more seconds by asking if you've stated it correctly. In responding, the questioner might offer information that makes the question clearer – and gives you more time to work on your response.

**Ask follow-up questions**. For example, ask "When you said … did you mean …?" In addition to buying time, follow-up questions generate additional information that may be useful.

**Ask a *how many of you* question**. For example, ask how many listeners can relate to the question. This tells you how many people are familiar with the subject and may be able to assist you in responding. And, oh yes, it buys you a few more seconds.

**Involve the audience.** I often tell the audience, "Before I give my answer, let's see what some of you think." Usually, several people offer comments, giving me a chance to gather my thoughts and offer my own perspective.

**Make an educated guess.** If you can make a reasonable guess, do so and explain that it's just a guess. Your response may satisfy the questioner or take the questioning in a different direction, redirecting attention from your lack of encyclopedic knowledge.

### Responding when you don't know the answer

**Be honest about not knowing.** People respect presenters who admit to not knowing – provided, of course, that this doesn't happen with *every* question. When I can't answer a question, I often ask if anyone in the audience can help, and usually, at least a few people can. I thank them and smile on the inside, knowing that I will now be better prepared to respond to the question in the future.

**Offer to follow-up.** If you don't know the answer, but suspect you can track it down, say so. Get the person's contact information and follow up. Getting back to the person will earn you credibility since many presenters who promise to follow up don't.

**Draw upon the expertise of a colleague.** If not being able to answer questions will be embarrassing, see if you can bring along a colleague who is strong where you're weak. Then you can simply turn to your colleague and ask, "Can you take this one?"

**Track the questions people ask**. Have a colleague record the questions or jot them down yourself when you're done. Every question may suggest information you can review so that you're ready to respond the next time someone asks the same question. It may even be information you can add to your next presentation.

## To recap

Fear about the ability to respond competently to audience questions is not unusual among technical professionals. If that's your situation:

- Anticipate possible questions and prepare responses so that you'll be able to handle those questions if they arise.
- When you're unsure of the answer, buy time by repeating the question, asking for clarification, or involving the audience.
- If you don't know the answer, be forthright about that fact, seek input from the audience or a colleague, and if appropriate, offer to follow up with the questioner.

## In conclusion

A response to a question is actually a mini-presentation and another opportunity to shine. The more questions you answer, the more fluent a presenter you'll become. If it's not already the case, you may soon find that addressing questions is one of the most energizing parts of presenting.

# CHAPTER 16: HOW TO MANAGE A DIFFICULT AUDIENCE

An occasional objection from an audience member is an opportunity to clarify a point the person may have missed or gain a new perspective by listening to the person's ideas. But it can be just plain tough, and even emotionally draining, to face customers, suppliers, senior managers, or even colleagues who vociferously disagree with you, constantly interrupt you, ruthlessly demean you, or in other ways, disrupt your presentation or treat you rudely. This chapter offers suggestions for managing these trying situations.

## When is a difficult audience not a difficult audience?

Once I label audience members as difficult, I find it harder to view them as reasonable people who may have a valid issue or complaint. I know I will be able to respond more effectively if I take them seriously, listen to their ideas, and try to understand their perspective. Therefore, when audience members raise issues in a vehement or vigorous manner, I try to think of them as a *challenging* audience, rather than a difficult audience.

Given this preference for *challenging* rather than *difficult*, why does the title of this chapter refer to a difficult audience? Simply because that's the term people use most often when describing a troublesome audience and I wanted you to be able to locate this chapter easily. But for the rest of this chapter, I'll use the term *challenging* rather than *difficult*.

## How to cope with a challenging audience

Fortunately, seriously challenging audiences are rare. Most audiences want you to succeed and treat you accordingly. And most of the time, you can be far from perfect in terms of presentation mechanics and they'll still treat you courteously.

Furthermore, sometimes you can take steps before a presentation to address the grievances of those who might otherwise use the presentation to sound off. But when challenging situations occur, what are your options?

**If you anticipate a challenging audience, prepare**. Learn what you can about the issues and concerns of those who will be in the audience. In presenting, do your best to stand tall and sound confident, no matter what they fling at you. Sometimes, they are simply trying to get you to cave in. Don't let that happen.

**Acknowledge how busy the audience is.** These days, so many people are overworked and stressed. Let them know at the outset that you appreciate their time constraints and respect their reality. Don't say anything that would suggest that you think you face more difficult circumstances than they do.

**Seek lighthearted ways to respond**. If the source of a disruption is relatively innocuous, aim for a lighthearted response. For example, if people are creating a distraction by whispering among themselves, show a slide of a photo taken at a hospital, along with the words "This is a quiet zone." Or use a sound-maker to recapture their attention; I use a set of jingle bells for this purpose. Or simply pause for a few moments; the silence usually causes them to quiet down.

**Treat challenging individuals directly.** If someone asks too many questions or long-winded questions, respond quickly and directly, such as by saying, "I appreciate that you have a lot of questions, but I'm going to move on now so everyone else has a chance to ask questions. I'll be available afterwards if you'd like to talk further." Most of the time, when an individual poses a challenge, everyone else in the audience is rooting for you and eager for you to respond in this way.

**Accept that audience anger may have a legitimate cause.** If, for example, customers suffered financial loss due to bugs in your latest release, you can't expect them to show up ready to party. If you know audience members are angry, try to meet with some of them one-on-one before your presentation to give them a chance to have their say. Get to know them. Discuss their concerns. Listen to them. In doing so, you may defuse some of their anger, making it less likely that they'll give you a hard time during your presentation.

**Watch your tone of voice**. This takes great presence of mind in challenging situations. But strive to maintain your composure and try not to sound like you're blaming the audience. Even if you believe they're at fault, keep your temper in check. Remember, anger begets even more anger; if you respond to their anger with your own, you'll have a difficult time regaining control. Conversely, if you remain calm (at least outwardly, even if you're tied in knots on the inside), people who are directing their anger at you will eventually calm down.

**Treat the audience with respect.** Being a presenter puts you in a position of authority, so no matter how the audience treats you, do your best to respond politely and empathetically. Don't dismiss anyone's concerns as trivial, because to the people who have these concerns, they are not trivial. Resist any temptation to speak to them in an arrogant, demeaning, or condescending manner.

**If audience members have been required to attend, tell them you know some of them would rather not be there.** Admitting this fact will win over some audience members and make them more receptive to your presentation. It's even possible that despite their initially negative attitude, your presentation will capture their interest.

**If audience members disagree with you, acknowledge their point of view.** Often, what people want more than anything is to have their views heard and acknowledged; once you've done that, you can usually present your own views without fear of attack.

**Take the offensive against audience negativity.** Some audiences delight in finding fault, as some of my colleagues have experienced in presenting to design or code review teams. If that's your situation, diminish the impact of their "attack" by explaining that you expect them to find flaws and you welcome their insights. This sends a signal that you're not going to let their flaw-finding run you down.

**Show respect for audience skepticism.** For example, when I give presentations on personality types to technical groups, I often encounter people who are dubious about personality differences. To minimize contentious reactions, I begin by asking how many people are skeptical about the topic. When people raise their hand, I tell them I appreciate such skepticism, and I encourage them to retain that perspective. This approach validates their views and increases the odds that if they raise objections, they'll do so in a considerate, non-disruptive manner.

**Consider your corporate culture.** You face a challenging situation if the management style in your organization is to demean or belittle the presenter. If that's the norm where you work, you might (when the job market permits) consider whether you want to work for such an organization. If you do, then the challenge is yours to be diligent in preparing your presentation and meeting management's expectations.

## To recap

Challenging audiences are the exception, not the rule. As usual, the starting point is to do your homework. Know your audience and be prepared to respond to their challenges. Treat their issues and complaints as legitimate. Acknowledge their perspective. Maintain your composure, no matter how they treat you.

If possible, seek to defuse audience members' anger and address their concerns before the presentation. That way, they may still not be pleased with what you're presenting, but they'll no longer be a challenge for you.

## In conclusion

As unnerving as it can be to face a challenging audience, doing so will help you improve as a presenter because you'll become increasingly proficient at responding. Not that you're likely to have many opportunities to gain this experience. Happily, most audiences will treat you respectfully.

# CHAPTER 17: HOW TO CONQUER NERVOUSNESS

If, despite the suggestions in the previous chapters, you still feel plagued by nervousness when you present – or even just think about presenting – you're not alone. Many people struggle to overcome their nervousness, including even some long-time presenters who consistently impress their audiences.

As you know, some nervousness when you're presenting is actually an energizer. But it's no fun to face an audience when your heart is pounding, your breathing is shallow, your palms are sweaty, and your knees are trembling. If your nervousness feels extreme, you may want to try some techniques that many people regularly practice to help them relax, reduce stress, sleep better, improve their health, and achieve a positive attitude. You may find these techniques worthwhile, even if you thrive on giving presentations and look forward to each one.

This chapter outlines several of these techniques, and describes how to use them in preparing for and giving a presentation. In particular:

- Practice deep breathing.
- Do qigong exercises.
- Eliminate stressors.
- Use visual imagery.
- Relive feelings of confidence.
- Mentally rehearse.
- Use positive affirmations.
- Create anchors.

## Practice deep breathing

When you become nervous, your breathing becomes shallow and rushed, which makes you even more nervous. Deep breathing releases tension and helps you relax. Note, however, that deep breathing doesn't mean sucking in the belly and raising the shoulders (the way many people breathe), but rather taking air deep into the belly while the chest remains still. If you place your hand on your abdomen and feel it expand when you inhale, you're on the right track.

Practice deep breathing on a regular basis, and particularly when you're working on an upcoming presentation. Also take a few minutes to do some deep breathing just before your presentation begins. That way, you'll begin in the calmest possible state.

## Do qigong exercises

One of my favorite ways to reduce stress is qigong (pronounced *chee gung*), an ancient Chinese practice that has become a modern relaxation technique. Qigong revolves around stretches, postures, and movements that seem too easy and gentle to have any effect at all. Nevertheless, by watching a video and following along for just 20 minutes, I become very relaxed.

As an alternative to qigong, or in addition to it, some people find yoga, tai chi, meditation, various forms of exercise, and other such practices effective in helping them feel calmer.

**Eliminate stressors**

What could be better than to eliminate all the stressors in your work and personal life? OK, maybe *all* is the wrong word. Obviously, many things that cause stress are outside your control, so start by focusing on stressors you *can* eliminate. The more relaxed you are when you're preparing for or giving a presentation, the less you'll be hounded by nervousness.

But you have choices even for things outside your control, because you can choose how you respond to them. One way to do this is to identify the positives in a negative situation. For example, instead of persistently venting that the recent project cancellation was a disastrous decision, reflect on what you learned during the project that you can transfer to your next project. Without pretending to be happy about the decision, you can change your perspective so that it has less of a negative effect on you.

**Use visual imagery**

This is a way to attain calmness by using your imagination to conjure up pleasing images. But the imagery is not just visual; in fact, you use all your senses. So, for example, if one of your happiest memories is of a hike you took along a mountain stream, close your eyes and visualize the stunning mountain scenery, hear the rushing water and chirping birds, smell the fragrant flowers along the trail, feel the gentle breeze, and taste the trail mix that you nibbled as you hiked. Yum!

Try using visual imagery for several minutes before practicing your presentation. Then, spend a few minutes going back to that pleasant place shortly before you present.

**Relive feelings of confidence**

This is similar to what actors do when they practice method acting, drawing from their own past experiences and emotions in order to give a realistic portrayal of the character they're playing.

In the context of presenting, the idea is to relive feelings of confidence by recalling situations or times when you felt confident and successful. What did your voice sound like? How did you stand? How did you walk? How did you interact with people? What was your facial expression? What was going on inside you? Then you try to summon those same feelings when you're practicing your presentation and again when you're delivering it.

If you like, think of it as play acting; you're playing the part of someone who is confident. You may even discover that it ceases to be a role you're playing and instead represents the real you.

## Mentally rehearse

With mental rehearsals, you imagine yourself successfully carrying out a specific activity. Competitive skiers, for example, close their eyes and visualize themselves racing the course – and winning.

For yourself, close your eyes and imagine yourself giving a superb presentation. Visualize yourself arriving at the presentation venue. Imagine yourself feeling strong and enthusiastic as you approach the podium. Listen to yourself sounding supremely confident as you begin your presentation. Visualize yourself enjoying yourself as you present. Imagine yourself looking out at your audience and seeing them listen to you with interest.

By creating a picture in your mind of how you look, sound and feel during a successful presentation, you will be creating a model that you can follow in the real thing. When you finally give the presentation, you will already have presented it several times in your mind, so you're just following in your own footsteps.

## Use positive affirmations

These are brief positive statements that you tell yourself to ward off negative beliefs. Positive affirmation for presenting might be, for example, "I am a strong, confident presenter" or "I give presentations that people enjoy" or "I thrive on public speaking." Positive affirmations are believed to reprogram your thinking by replacing negative beliefs with positive ones.

Some people think positive affirmations are silly; other people find them highly effective. If your nervousness is overwhelming, you've got nothing to lose by giving them a try. By repeating positive affirmations to yourself, *with conviction*, during your practice sessions and just before you present, you may find that you've reduced your troubling level of anxiety to a normal dose of nervousness.

## Create anchors

Anchoring is a form of conditioning in which you associate something, such as a gesture, object, or sound (an external stimulus), with a certain thought, mood, state of mind, or emotion (an internal response). For example, you might touch the wrist of your left hand with your right hand whenever you're feeling particularly calm.

By repeatedly using this touch whenever you feel calm, you're creating a connection. Then if you become nervous while presenting, touching your wrist in the same way may generate that same feeling of calmness – and no one will notice.

Another type of anchor that can be useful in presenting is a small object, such as a small stone, that you associate with the calm state you want to feel while presenting. By keeping it in your pocket and touching it once or twice as you present, you can trigger that feeling of calmness.

It may take time to create a connection between the external stimulus and your desired internal response, so begin working on it well before your presentation.

## Put it all together for the presentation

Shortly before you present, find a quite place where you can spend a few minutes by yourself. Sit down, close your eyes, breathe deeply, summon the imagery that you found most effective during your practice sessions, give yourself some positive affirmations, and try to relax.

As you present, strive to maintain a feeling of calmness. If you feel nervous, simply notice that nervousness and let it be, recognizing that it's actually helping you give a more dynamic presentation.

If your nervousness threatens to undermine your presentation, periodically pause and take some deep breaths. Speak a little slower and louder; projecting your voice will mask the nervousness. Recall that feeling of confidence you experienced during practice. Tell yourself that you're doing just fine; the odds are in your favor that you really are.

As a practical matter, if you feel especially nervous, don't hold any paper in your hand or it'll flutter and call attention to your nervousness. If you have a glass of water nearby, keep it far enough away that you don't knock it over. (And don't put it on your laptop!)

Remember, it's best not to announce that you're nervous. Despite how disconcerting it feels, the audience may be unaware of it.

As a reminder, do *not* use drugs, alcohol, medication, or anything else to calm you down (or perk you up) before you present. The one time I violated this advice, I drank some wine at a dinner meeting. I wasn't nervous; I just (foolishly) thought, why not? During my presentation, I felt like I had to search for every third syllable. No one commented on it afterwards, so maybe my sputtering was all in my mind. Still, it's just not worth the risk.

## To recap

If you're nagged by nervousness before or during a presentation, techniques that may help you get it under control include:

- deep breathing
- qigong, yoga, meditation, exercise
- stress reduction
- visual imagery
- method acting (or play acting)
- mental rehearsals
- positive affirmations
- anchoring.

I've barely scratched the surface in describing these techniques. Do a Web search for any of them for a lot more detail.


## In conclusion

Are there any downsides to these techniques? Sure. You might fall asleep doing them. When I try to use visual imagery, I don't see myself hiking along a mountain stream; I see ... nothing ... because I've slipped into nap-land. Still, if that happens to you, it's not so bad – as long as it doesn't happen while you're presenting. (Another good reason to stand while presenting; there's less chance you'll fall asleep.)

# PART V: TIPS FOR SELECTED CONTEXTS

This section offers tips for seven specific presentation contexts. Everything in previous chapters is relevant here, but these contexts call for some additional attention.

**Chapter 18, Presenting to management**, helps you have a strong, positive impact when presenting to your superiors.

**Chapter 19, Presenting to customers**, emphasizes things you should keep in mind, given that your customers see things differently than you do.

**Chapter 20, Presenting to your team**, offers tips for presenting to your teammates, whether they attend in person or are geographically dispersed.

**Chapter 21, Presenting to a foreign audience**, guides you in presenting to an audience in which some or all aren't fluent in your language.

**Chapter 22, Presenting at conferences**, explains how to be invited to present at conferences and what to expect in presenting at them.

**Chapter 23, Presenting webinars**, provides tips for presenting in this increasingly common presentation format.

**Chapter 24, Presenting with co-presenters**, offers ideas for presenting with colleagues, customers, or anyone else.

# CHAPTER 18: PRESENTING TO MANAGEMENT

While everything in the preceding chapters is relevant in presenting to management, there are some additional things that you'll want to keep in mind. This chapter focuses on tips for presenting to anyone from your immediate boss to the CEO and board of directors. If they're higher in rank than you, the following tips apply:

- Tailor your presentation to their perspective.
- Get to the point.
- Incorporate an appropriate level of complexity.
- Accommodate their communication preferences.
- Be cautious about using humor.
- Anticipate possible questions and objections.
- Rehearse.

## Tailor your presentation to their perspective

Presentations to management are typically for the purpose of informing and persuading. The key to successfully informing or persuading is to consider your audience's perspective. In the case of your management, what do they need to know or do to be successful – and to be *perceived* as successful by their own superiors? What do *you* need to know to put your presentation in their terms?

Consider, for example, the IT director who sought the go-ahead from top management for a major acquisition. He drew three boxes on the white board and told the assembled executives, "Here are three boxes. Let's label them X, Y, and Z. You don't need to be concerned with what they do.

The important thing is what they will enable you to accomplish."

He then gave a presentation that focused on the acquisition in terms of management's top priorities. He left the meeting with the funding and approval to proceed.

In preparing to present to management, consider their priorities, pressures, fears, and frustrations. What drives their key decisions? Reducing costs? Improving on-time delivery? Increasing customer satisfaction? Overcoming a negative public image? Doing more with less? Learn what's important to those you're presenting to and tailor your presentation accordingly.

**Get to the point**

Don't pontificate. Synonyms for pontification in my online thesaurus include *sound off, preach, go on,* and *hold forth* – all things to avoid doing in presenting to your superiors. As busy people with numerous competing priorities, they are in a position to stop you half-way through if they don't find your material relevant and compelling. Therefore, stick to what's important and omit the rest.

Keep in mind the inverted pyramid approach (or inverted triangle, as it's often drawn). This refers to presenting the most important information first and then successively less important material.

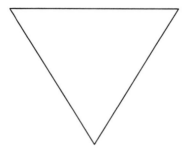

This approach, which derives from the newspaper industry, is based on the realization that most people don't read a newspaper article beyond the first few paragraphs. With the most important information at the top, readers can quickly glean the essential information. In addition, if space originally intended for the article is needed for an ad or a breaking story, editors can cut from the end without being concerned about slashing critical information.

This same idea applies to presenting to management. Something may come up that requires them to make an early exit. Therefore, begin with your conclusion and then provide supporting information, going from most important to least important. That way, even if circumstances prevent you from giving the entire presentation, they'll at least have heard your most important information.

**Incorporate an appropriate level of complexity**

Having urged you in Chapter 9 to minimize the use of text-filled slides, I now offer a possible exception based on a personal experience. I was once invited to speak at an executive retreat that my client, a high-tech company, was holding for its customers, senior managers of technology divisions. Dean, the director who invited me, assigned a graphic artist to design slides for my presentation. In each of the resulting slides was a few words to make the key point, plus a whimsical cartoon that supported that point.

Dean reviewed my presentation and slides and signed off on both. I knew my slides would be a big hit. I was wrong.

It quickly became evident from the executives' comments and facial expressions that they found my slides too simplistic. The next presenter's slides, which were filled with complex charts and tiny type, apparently met their expectations of what constituted executive-oriented slides. The audience loved his presentation.

My takeaway is that what will appeal to the audience takes priority over seemingly sound guidelines. If I had included a few slides that conveyed complexity, I might have squeaked by. Now I know.

**Accommodate their communication preferences**

This suggestion may not be practical if you're presenting to a large audience, but if you're presenting to just one or two individuals or a small group, consider how they like to receive information. Do they favor colorful charts and graphs? Visual images? Text? Statistics?

Do they prefer to view slides or read printed information? Do they prefer high-level or in-depth information? And relative to the simplicity/complexity issue, would it be smarter to keep your slides simple or make them look complex?

When I was an IT manager, our new director didn't want formal presentations. He was a let's-get-on-with-it guy. If we couldn't give him the facts swiftly and concisely, he wasn't interested. Look at slides? Not a chance. His communication preferences were altogether different from his bullet-point-driven predecessor. We quickly learned that we had to change our ways to accommodate his.

Think about what you know about the communication preferences of those you'll be presenting to, and seek input from colleagues. Tailoring your presentation to their preferences may make them more receptive to your information than they might otherwise be.

## Be cautious about using humor

This applies to all audiences, of course, but it's especially important in presenting to upper management. Why? Because they may take themselves seriously – or at least want to be *seen* as taking themselves seriously. As a result, they may not find your humor amusing, even if they'd find it uproariously funny if they heard it from one of their peers. If they already know you and they appreciate your light-hearted approach to serious issues, then go for it. Otherwise, use caution.

I'm certainly not implying that senior managers are humorless nor would I insist that you never use humor in presenting to them. Just think twice before you do so. Or maybe three or four times.

### Anticipate possible questions and objections

If you can't answer a question while presenting to your co-workers, it's not the end of the world. If you can't answer a question while presenting to your superiors, the end of the world may be a bit closer than you'd like. Therefore, contemplate the questions they might ask and make very sure you can respond.

If you're making a proposal, or seeking backing for a project, prepare to respond to objections. To do this, take a position opposed to the case you're making and identify – and write down – all the objections you can. This isn't easy to do; after all, you're arguing against your own interests. But by identifying possible objections, you can formulate ways to counter them. In the process, you may be able to strengthen your case by weeding out flaws and weaknesses.

Several technology managers have asked me whether it's better to anticipate questions and answer them *before* anyone asks them or hold back in order to respond competently *if* someone asks. In a presentation to management, it's usually better to be forthcoming. If you withhold key information in anticipation of a question, your listeners may see you as unprepared. Why, the executive might wonder, did you not provide this information without my having to ask?

Of course, if it's a point that might damage your persuasive case, and it's a point your audience is unlikely to ask about, maybe (just maybe) it's worth holding back.


### Rehearse

Rehearsing is crucial for presentations to a company's top officials. People who give presentations to this level often hold numerous rehearsals, tweaking every slide, reviewing every point, practicing the entire presentation, and giving special attention to any part that seems weak.

A great strength of many technical professionals is they have a vast body of knowledge that they're often eager to share. But this strength can turn into a problem if you're giving a presentation that requires that you adhere closely to an agreed agenda. A CIO had recently given a presentation to a board of directors to seek funding; he told me how critical it was that he and his team should stick to their script and not make impromptu remarks that could undermine their message.

**To recap**

In preparing to present to management, consider their issues and concerns, their fears and frustrations, their priorities and pressures, and their communication preferences, and tailor your presentation accordingly. In particular:

- Frame your presentation in terms of their perspective.
- Present the most important information first.
- Make sure your material is appropriately complex.
- Accommodate their communication preferences.
- Be cautious about using humor.
- Prepare to respond to possible questions and objections.
- Practice and practice some more.

These issues are important in presenting to all levels of management, but the higher up they are, the more important these issues become.

## In conclusion

Management can be a tough audience, especially if your goal is to persuade. To the extent feasible, build credibility in advance so that when you present, you will receive a fair hearing. Never underestimate the power of your reputation to give you an advantage when you present to management.

# CHAPTER 19: PRESENTING TO CUSTOMERS

Whether your customers are business units to whom you provide services and support, companies to whom you sell products and services, or colleagues down the hall (or half a world away), their perspective as customers is likely to differ from your own. As a result, when you present to them, they may hear things differently from what you intended.

Given this potential for misunderstanding, this chapter offers the following tips:

- Consider your customers' perspective.
- Guard against potentially ambiguous terminology.
- Show that you understand their business.
- Watch your attitude.
- Allow ample time for questions.
- Be careful how you sell.
- Remember that appearances count.

## Consider your customers' perspective

As an IT project manager, I learned the hard way that what you call something matters. My project team had created a system for a large customer division. A major unit of the division, known by the acronym *BOC*, handled 75% of the transactions that flowed through the division. Accordingly, the developers used BOC to identify the segments of the system associated with this unit.

Three small units in the division handled the remaining 25% of the transactions. The logic associated with these three units was identical, but different from the logic for the BOC unit. For convenience, the developers used *NONBOC* for the segments of the system related to these three units.

When the system was almost completed, we gave a presentation to key members of the division. Upon seeing a slide that displayed an overview of the system and included the term *NONBOC*, a manager of one of the three small units bolted out of her chair and exclaimed, "How dare you describe us in terms of what we aren't!"

To the managers of the three small units, this naming convention was no trivial matter. Having responsibility for tasks that were fewer in number and of less impact than those of the BOC team, they were sensitive to their status in the division. And there we were calling attention to it.

We had blundered, not in our naming conventions – they'd never see the code, after all – but in blithely displaying terminology in our presentation without considering how it would sound to our customers.

Take care to avoid situations like this. Consider your customers' perspective in the information you present.

## Guard against potentially ambiguous terminology

Terminology, by its very nature, is ambiguous. Just ask Christopher, an IT manager. When Deb, his customer, asked him for a status report on the system his team was developing, he created a brief presentation. Upon viewing slides filled with timelines, milestone markers, and tiny triangles, circles, diamonds, and squares, she exclaimed "That's not a status report. It's gibberish!"

*Status report* may not sound like a potentially ambiguous term, but it is. In fact, it's an example of terminology that's so familiar that you probably use it routinely. Yet such terminology might mean something different to your customers than it means to you.

In addition to *status report*, consider such potentially ambiguous terms as *project, problem, respond,* and *resolve.* Before you give a presentation to customers, ask yourself how they might misinterpret what you say. Pay particular attention to acronyms, which may stand for something altogether different to your customers than to you.

Before presenting to customers, you might want to give your presentation to a colleague who takes the role of a customer and challenges your terminology. Or pilot the presentation with customers who represent those you will be presenting to.

### Show that you understand their business

A complaint I've often heard from customers is that the people who support their needs don't understand their business. For example, I spoke to a customer who grumbled that the IT staff persisted in talking network nonsense (her term). "I don't know what they're talking about," she complained. "I work in a world of assets, expenses and spreadsheets, not bandwidth and apps and mips and blips" (also her terms).

Customers want the technical personnel who support their needs to know their language (business-speak, in other words) and to use that language in providing explanations, justifications, and rationales. If you're going to present to customers, make sure you have at least a rudimentary knowledge of their terminology and the ability to use it in a meaningful manner. Strive to incorporate their jargon into your presentations and minimize use of your own.

## Watch your attitude

Sam, a security manager, gave a presentation to alert customers to the potential security breaches the company faced. He explained that his job was to ensure the safety and confidentiality of the company's data. The company had had one serious breach and couldn't afford another. But what a condescending tone of voice!

Sam might as well have said, "Now, now, boys and girls, you're not smart enough to understand this, but I'll do my best to get through to you." As Sam spoke, customers looked increasingly annoyed.

Sam's tone of voice did him a disservice. What's worse, while customers might otherwise have taken Sam's information seriously, it seemed likely that under these offensive circumstances, many would dismiss or ignore his advice. Many, I'm certain, would have walked out if their management hadn't directed them to attend.

Your attitude conveys a strong message about what you think of your listeners, and their receptiveness to your information will hinge on that attitude. If you think little of your audience, keep it to yourself. Make sure the attitude they notice is positive and respectful.

## Allow ample time for questions

Gretchen, an IT director, presented a technology overview to several business units. Before she began, she urged people to ask questions at any point. Then she launched into a fast-paced, pause-free presentation. She later told me she couldn't understand why there were no questions.

If you're willing to take questions during your presentation, pause at intervals and explicitly invite questions. Then give people a chance to respond.

Recognize that in the presence of technical people, non-technical customers may fear that they will sound ignorant if they ask questions. Therefore, you might want to give them other ways to submit questions, such as writing them down and forwarding them to a colleague who will ask them on behalf of the group. Or encourage listeners to submit questions by e-mail after the presentation.

## Be careful how you sell

How you sell is as important as what you sell. For example, you can lose a sale by giving a presentation that aggressively pursues a sale without first building a relationship with key customers.

Some customers feel threatened by anything that's new or different. The bigger the decision, the longer the sale is likely to take, so don't expect your presentation to achieve the impossible. The key is patient persistence.

Sometimes, the customers' superiors need to see the merits of the case. In other words, your customers may need to make a sale before you can make one yourself. So the key to your success is to find out what you can do to help them prepare a persuasive presentation to their superiors.

**Remember that appearances count**

Eric Bloom, author of *Manager Mechanics*, told me about a sales representative who was reviewing his e-mail while his colleagues presented to customers. What kind of impression do you suppose that made on customers? When you're part of a team that is presenting to customers, you're on stage whether or not you you're the one presenting.

**To recap**

In preparing a presentation for customers:

- Put on your customer hat and try to imagine the world as they experience it.
- Diligently search for potentially ambiguous terms.
- Speak so that it's clear you understand their business.
- Be mindful of the attitude you're communicating.
- If you invite questions, allow time for people to ask them.
- Stay focused when colleagues are presenting.

**In conclusion**

At work you're a customer to your suppliers and vendors. You're also a customer as you make your daily rounds outside of work. When you think about presentations you've attended as a customer, what pleased you? What drove you to the boiling point and beyond? Use these insights in preparing to present to your own customers.

# CHAPTER 20: PRESENTING TO YOUR TEAM

Presentations to management or customers tend to be high-pressure situations. By contrast, presentations to your team are an opportunity to present with a minimum of pressure and formality. This chapter offers tips for presenting to team members when they can all be physically present, as well as when they are geographically dispersed.

## Benefits of presenting to your team

If you're apprehensive about giving formal presentations, presenting to your team is an excellent way to gain experience in a non-threatening setting. Topics abound: demonstrating a clever technique, proposing a new project, providing an update on meetings you attended, describing what you learned at a recent conference, and much more.

One team I visited had a different team member give a brief presentation each month. This gave everyone a chance to get some practice presenting, while also sharing useful information.

Whether or not you yearn to present to your team, doing so can help you build a reputation as a confident presenter, which can increase your credibility, clout, and career options.

## Presentation anxiety, team-style

Some people are fine presenting to people they know, but lose sleep over presenting to people they don't know. Other people are fine speaking to people they don't know, but they're a bundle of nerves presenting to their peers.

Of the two, I think the latter is more common. We'd rather not have either audience view us as incompetent, but if it's a choice, we'd rather have strangers see us as incompetent than the people we work with every day.

If presenting to your team makes you nervous, preparation (as always) is the key.

- Get your presentation ready as far in advance as you can.
- Rehearse it.
- If possible, present it to a colleague, perhaps someone in another department.
- Plan ahead for the equipment and material you'll need to bring with you.
- Familiarize yourself with the room you'll be presenting in.
- Anticipate questions and objections.

And so on. In other words, draw from the suggestions in this book.

**Presentations to on-site teams**

These tips pertain to presentations when all team members can attend in person.

**Format**: Presentations to your team are likely to be shorter than other presentations, perhaps closer to 20 to 30 minutes than 90. You may not need to open with an agenda if the topic is a recurring one. There's no need for an introduction, unless new members have joined the team since the last gathering. Given that you're presenting to your co-workers, you can wear whatever you'd normally wear.

**Setting**: Will the team meet in an office? A meeting room? An off-site location? Try to arrange a setting in which the space is appropriate for the number of people attending. Presenting to four team members in a gigantic auditorium is an energy-zapper for both the presenter and the audience. (A dozen people in a cubicle is no fun either!)

**Seating arrangement**: In the ideal setting, team members are seated in a circle or around a table so that everyone can see each other. This type of setting contributes to the air of informality that's lacking when people are seated in rows and the view that most have is of the back of the heads in front of them. If the team is too large to fit around a conference room table, you may be able to arrange seating so that everyone can see at least several others.

**Standing vs. sitting**: Whereas it's usually more effective to stand when you present to a large group, it's up to you whether you stand or sit for a presentation to your team. Sitting may seem more natural in a small space with only a few people. Standing may be more comfortable if you're periodically jotting pointers on a flipchart. I feel more energetic when I present standing, so that's usually my preference. Do whatever is most comfortable for you.

**Timing**: Although the setting may be informal, you still have to make sure you can cover what you need to in the time allotted, including time for questions and discussion. Keep in mind that planning a short presentation can be harder than planning a long one because you have to carefully select what to include and what to omit. Whether it's 10 minutes or an hour, make sure you'll be able to end on time.

**Slides**: You can probably keep your slides simpler than if you're trying to impress a high-stakes audience. In one company I consulted to, all IT employees had laptops which they brought to meetings with them. Presentation material was distributed in advance and people viewed it on their laptops during the presentation. But you may be able to skip slides altogether unless the subject matter requires everyone to look at certain information at the same time. Even then, a handout may suffice.

**Interaction**: In a formal presentation, you have to decide what kinds of interaction to include. Presentations to a team, by contrast, lend themselves to an easy-flowing give and take, with questions, comments, and discussion throughout, as well as a simulation or team activity if it fits your topic. The presentation is likely to feel closer to a conversation than to a formal presentation.

**Ground rules**: Beware: if team members have a lot of opinions, the relative informality of the setting can cause you to lose control over your material and your timing. Therefore, ground rules may be appropriate. For example, if interruptions will divert you from your main points, ask people to hold their comments until the end. If you're concerned that they'll veer into an unrelated issue that's been troubling them, be explicit at the outset that the topic is not part of your presentation.

**Presentations to geographically dispersed teams**

Nothing can replace face-to-face interaction. But for geographically dispersed teams, in-person meetings are infrequent. Even teams in which team members are only a few miles apart are increasingly holding virtual meetings to save back-and-forth time.

When I presented to a team in which most team members worked in the building where I was presenting, I was surprised to discover that the others (who I'd been told worked at a remote location) were a mere three blocks away. I would have preferred for them to be present; they clearly preferred to stay where they were and call in.

In giving a presentation in which members of the team are in different locations, keep in mind the following:

**Check-in.** If team members are in multiple locations and the team is small, start by having them identify themselves and give their location. That way, everyone knows who is attending.

**Tone of voice.** Listening to a disembodied voice can be mind-numbing, so aim to sound lively and conversational. Imagine that you're speaking to a friend about a topic you're both enthused about.

**Material.** If possible, prepare slides or written material so that people have something to look at as they listen. Distribute whatever material you can in advance so people have it handy at show time.

**Structure**. Provide more structure than you might for a presentation, in which you and your audience can see each other. For example, start by listing the topics you'll be talking about. When you begin the first topic, identify it as the first, talk about it, be explicit when you're concluding that topic, and state that you're now moving to the second topic. Make sure that listeners can keep track of where you are in the presentation.

**Audio-visual preparations**. Check in advance to be sure any A/V or communication equipment you'll be using is in working order. Make sure team members understand how to access the presentation. If circumstances conspire to prevent you from starting on time, do your best to end at the agreed upon time.

**Audience involvement**. If you're using a set-up that enables listeners to speak to you, ask questions and try to involve them. Some managers who present to remote teams like to call on people to respond to various issues. If you like this idea, you might want to alert people in advance that you will be calling on them so they can be prepared – unless not forewarning them is a deliberate strategy so that everyone stays alert (or at least awake).

**Q&A.** Allow ample time for questions both during the presentation and at the end. Have listeners who comment or ask questions identify themselves so that others know who's talking. Stating their location is also a good idea if they are in several different locations.

**Scheduling**. If team members are in multiple time zones, select a time that is reasonable for the majority of them. But if you give presentations to the team regularly, vary the presentation time so the same team members don't always have to attend at an inconvenient time.

**Language and cultural differences**. When people are in different countries, or different parts of the same country, language and cultural differences are likely. Therefore, minimize the use of local slang and be careful about words that mean different things in different locations. See the next chapter for related tips for presenting to foreign audiences.

**Duration**. Keep the presentation brief – preferably no more than 20–30 minutes, unless you positively need more time to do a thorough job. Keeping people engaged when they can't see you is a challenge in the best of cases.

**Co-presenting**. If feasible, have someone else give part of the presentation. This gives listeners a chance to hear two different voices and styles of speaking.

**Action items**. If you'll be assigning action items, state explicitly who is to do what and by when.

**Follow-up**. Document any decisions made, actions taken, or issues addressed during the presentation and distribute this information as quickly as possible after the presentation.


**To recap**

Presentations to a team may be much more informal than presentations to other audiences, and therefore easier to prepare and less pressured to deliver.

When team members can all attend the presentation in person, you can adjust the format, setting, seating arrangement, interaction, use of slides, and other details to accommodate the relative informality.

A presentation to a geographically dispersed team is a bigger challenge and needs special attention to such details as presentation structure, written materials, scheduling, audio-visual preparations, and geographical or cultural differences among team members.

Many of the tips for presenting webinars (Chapter 23) are also relevant in presenting to a dispersed team.

**In conclusion**

Several people whom I asked about tips for presenting to teams said, "Food works!" Of course! Though whether you provide carrots and celery sticks or delectable, scrumptious, mouth-watering pastries and pies could make a difference in how listeners rate the presentation.

# CHAPTER 21: PRESENTING TO A FOREIGN AUDIENCE

You're giving a presentation you've given many times to your colleagues. But this time listeners are staring at you, as if they don't understand a word you're saying. What's going on?

It could be that they *don't* understand if the language you're speaking isn't their native language. Given the global nature of so many companies and the prevalence of geographically dispersed teams, the odds are good that you will some day give a presentation to people whose native language is not your own. This chapter offers tips for presenting in these circumstances.

## Language and cultural differences

When the native language of the audience differs from yours, they may not understand the slang, idioms, and colloquialisms in your presentation, so it's best to avoid them.

Actually, this is *much* easier said than done: these speech patterns are so familiar that we don't realize we're using them. Don't make a mountain out of a molehill (an example of an idiom that may not translate well). I could care less (an example of a colloquialism that we use when we actually mean *I couldn't care less.*) Too much slang is a red flag (and that's an idiom).

Do a Web search for *slang*, *idioms*, and *colloquialisms* for long lists of examples. Review your presentation for any such speech patterns and replace them with more direct language.

In addition, when you use acronyms or technical terms that people may not know, explain them. But be equally careful with non-technical terms. In a keynote presentation to a European audience on managing change, I said that people's responses to major change are sometimes more emotional and visceral than logical and rational. Afterwards, an audience member asked me the meaning of *visceral*. I should have realized that this word might be obscure to some listeners.

Of course, you can have problems being understood even when your audience speaks the same language you do. When I started giving presentations in the UK, the Web was not yet available to help me translate American English into British English, so I created my own English-to-English dictionary. Here's a sample:

| British English | American English |
|:---:|:---:|
| bobby | policeman |
| bonnet | hood of a car |
| chemist's | drug store |
| dear | expensive |
| first floor | second floor |
| left luggage | baggage room |
| nappy | diaper |
| roundabout | traffic circle |
| underground | subway |
| zed | z |

I routinely tell my UK audiences, "If anything I say in my presentation sounds inappropriate or offensive, I assure you that's not my intention. It is simply that I'm speaking my

English rather than yours. I appreciate your feedback so I can get better at speaking *your* English."

In fact, with my book, *Changing How You Manage and Communicate Change* (published, like this one, by UK-based IT Governance Publishing), we had an amusing time during the editing process in meshing my American English and my publisher's British English. I expect the same will happen with this book.

## Cultural differences that create misunderstanding

Cultural differences may also account for listeners seeming not to understand you. When I gave a presentation at a software conference in Tokyo, an interpreter translated my remarks into Japanese. Nevertheless, the audience stared, expressionless. They obviously didn't like my material.

Afterwards, to my surprise, several people graciously thanked me and commented on specific points I had made. Their English was imperfect, but much better than my Japanese.

I subsequently learned that Japanese audiences tend to listen to speakers quietly and respectfully. They may not be displaying visible reactions, but they're paying close attention. They understood my presentation just fine. I was the one who didn't understand. What I learned from that experience is that it's important to do your homework before speaking to a foreign audience so as to be prepared for differences of this kind.

**Parlez-vous français?**

Here are some additional tips for successfully presenting to audience members who aren't fluent in your language. These tips apply as well when audience members are from regions of your country where they speak your language but with its own idiosyncrasies and jargon.

**Monitor your pace**. Whatever your natural pace, slow down. If it'll help you remember, write yourself a *slow down* note that you can see as you're presenting.

**Enunciate.** When people aren't fluent in your language, they can have a hard time distinguishing where one word ends and the next one begins. Make a point of speaking precisely and distinctly.

**Periodically pause for a few seconds.** Pausing is important in all presentations, but people who aren't fluent in your language especially need a chance to absorb your message.

**Use visuals to support your presentation**. Slides or handouts give listeners an additional way to take in your information. With access to your information in both spoken and written forms, they'll be better able to understand what you're presenting.

**Be careful about your gestures**. *Exceedingly* careful. Some gestures that may be commonplace in your country or culture may mean something offensive or insulting in another country or culture. This applies to non-verbals as seemingly innocent as holding your palm, fist or arm in a certain position or even just pointing your finger. Do a Web search for *offensive gestures* for examples, photos and illustrations.

**Learn about cultural or national customs**. For example, when I presented a seminar in Hong Kong, we were treated to a lavish multi-course lunch, a local custom as I discovered. Everyone was stuffed by the end. For my next visit, I rearranged my material so as to present information-intensive content into the morning and lighter content après-lunch.

**Be careful in using humor**. Some humor is universal. Much more is culture-specific or language-specific. Before you use humor, make sure it translates well. Get feedback from people familiar with the language and culture so you know what to keep and what to discard.

**Acknowledge the language of your listeners**. If you can, incorporate a bit of their language into your presentation. I like to open my presentations in the language of the country I'm visiting. It takes extra preparation but their surprise and delight makes it worth it. I don't worry about getting it just right, because listeners appreciate the effort.

**Be sensitive to your audience's cultural background.** Agile coach, Jutta Eckstein, told me about an American speaking to a western European audience who used examples from the military to make his point, a mistake in the view of that audience. Think about who your audience is and draw examples from their culture and experience.

**To succeed with these suggestions, get feedback on your presentation *before* you give it**. Consider writing it out and requesting feedback from colleagues who speak the language(s) of those who will be in your audience. If that's too much work, select specific sentences or ideas that you'll be presenting and seek feedback.

## When the presenter is a non-native speaker

Some technical professionals whose native language is not English have told me they are concerned that listeners won't understand their accent. If that's your situation, consider the advice of Miquel Casas, a change artist, who learned that because he has an accent, people are likely to listen more carefully. In other words, an accent can actually be an advantage.

Miquel has fun with his accent. At the beginning of a presentation, he often says something like: "I have a different accent and I don't know where it came from, but if you don't understand something, please feel free to raise your hand and ask, and I will repeat in English." People laugh and he can then give the presentation without concern for his accent.

## To recap

In preparing a presentation for listeners who may not be fluent in your language:

- Learn all you can about relevant national and cultural differences.
- Evaluate your terminology, concepts and gestures to reduce the odds of baffling or offending your audience.
- Get feedback to help you weed out subtle ambiguities.
- Monitor your pace and pauses as you present.

- Use slides to give audience members a visual means of taking in your information.

## In conclusion

You may find that the additional attention to detail that's necessary in preparing to present to a foreign audience helps you do better with presentations to all your other audiences. That's been my experience.

# CHAPTER 22: PRESENTING AT CONFERENCES

Speaking at an international, national, regional, or local conference can significantly enhance your credibility, clout, and professional status. It's an opportunity to share your insights, convey useful information, and gain a reputation as an expert in your topic. And it's where many technical professionals get their start in public speaking.

Here's what's exciting about presenting at conferences. Many other presenters will exhibit the attributes of the worst presentations, as outlined in Chapter 3. They'll move around too much. They'll face the screen. They'll avoid eye contact. They'll omit interaction. They'll display text-filled slides and immediately begin talking, oblivious to the fact that people can't read the slides and listen to them at the same time.

You, who know better, will stand out as poised, prepared, and professional.

This chapter addresses the following tips:

- Identify conferences where you might present.
- Submit a proposal to present.
- Meet your deadlines.
- Be on site early.
- Be careful setting up.
- Chat with audience members.
- Don't be distracted by people who walk out.
- Respond to questions astutely.
- Behave professionally at all times.
- Thank the conference director.

## Identify conferences where you might present

Conferences run the gamut from 60 attendees and four 90-minute sessions to several thousand attendees and hundreds of sessions spread over several days, with many sessions run concurrently.

You can learn about conference possibilities by talking to colleagues and scanning online and print publications that address your topic. In addition, if you do a Web search for, for example, *software conferences*, you'll find links to numerous conferences. The best way to know if a specific conference is one you'd like to speak at is to attend it yourself – if you're fortunate enough to have your company send you.

## Submit a proposal to present

Most conferences require you to submit a proposal, describing your presentation topic and your background. Be aware that the proposal form, which is usually available on the conference website, is typically due many months before the conference. That gives conference staff time to review proposals, select presenters, and create promotional material well ahead of the conference date.

Be forewarned that many conferences receive hundreds of proposals and the selection process is laborious. If your proposal isn't accepted the first time you try, it's worth resubmitting the next time around. Or try a different topic. Or submit multiple proposals. Sometimes, one topic will appeal to the selection team more than another. And sometimes, they'll invite you to give more than one presentation.

## Meet your deadlines

When you're invited to present, you'll typically be notified about various deadlines, such as for submitting your slides (usually in pdf format). As much as you might like to work on your slides right up to the last minute, many conferences require your slide images months in advance to allow time to create the conference proceedings for attendees.

If you ask conference administrators what drives them crazy, high on the list will be presenters who don't meet their deadlines. Don't be one of them; in fact, do just the reverse and respond well ahead of the deadline. Presenters so rarely deliver requested material ahead of time that you will stand out from all the rest as someone who is easy to work with.

## Be on site early

That way, you can check out the room you'll be presenting in, tend to any last-minute logistical matters, and make sure you have everything you need.

Notice who or what precedes you on the agenda. The ideal is to be the first presenter of the day or in the first time slot after lunch. That way, you'll have time to get set up while the room is empty. If you follow another speaker, find out how much time you have between that person's ending time and your starting time; 15 to 30 minutes is the most common.

Give yourself enough time to have your equipment set up and ready to go, so you can chat with audience members and begin in a relaxed frame of mind.

## Be careful setting up

This is a tip I wouldn't have thought to mention until the unthinkable almost happened. A few years ago, at a US conference, I started unpacking my laptop as the previous presenter put his away. As he headed out on his way to the airport to fly back to Zurich, his home, I tried to plug my power cord into my computer and discovered – what? – it didn't plug in. He had grabbed my power cord, thinking it was his, and I was left with his! And he was leaving the country!

I caught him seconds before he reached the door. Gulp!

I guess the lesson is to pay attention. Don't get distracted talking to people. And keep your distance as the previous speaker packs up. I will *not* let this one happen to me again!

## Chat with audience members

Even if you're an experienced presenter who's comfortable strolling into the room moments before the starting time, it's a good idea to arrive early to connect with audience members. People form impressions quickly; by interacting with a few of them, you'll come across as friendly and interested, not just with the people you're chatting with, but with all others who see or hear you.

If you're the sort who isn't crazy about making small talk, identify one or two people (look for a few friendly faces), and chat with them. Ask where they're from. Ask what they think of the conference so far. Ask what kinds of challenges they face relative to your presentation topic.

## Don't be distracted by people who walk out

As you present, you may see some people walking out. It could be that they're unhappy with your presentation. But they may simply have decided that your presentation wasn't what they were looking for, and they'd prefer to attend a different session. It could also be that they need to catch a plane. Or they reached a state of information overload and need a nap.

Try to ignore these departures. Or state at the beginning, as I sometimes do, "I know you have many sessions to choose from. If, at any point, you decide this isn't the right session for you, please feel free to leave and try another session." That saves both them and me from feeling awkward when they leave.

## Respond to questions astutely

When audience members ask questions, repeat them before responding for anyone who couldn't hear them. Repeating questions also ensures that people attending remotely have heard them; increasingly, conferences are making "virtual" attendance possible by arranging for sessions to be presented in a webinar or webcast format, which enables people to "attend" online.

As you respond to questions, keep an eye on the time. If another presenter follows you and you weren't able to get to some people's questions, offer to talk with them afterwards outside the meeting room or later on during the conference. It's irksome to have a presenter run overtime, leaving the next presenter too little to get set up.

## Behave professionally at all times

As a conference presenter, you are among the select few who have been invited to share your information with an audience. This is an esteemed role and people see you as an expert and an authority in your field. That means that your reputation hinges not just on how you perform when you are presenting, but also how you behave when you're not.

For most presenters, this is a no-brainer; simply be who you are on stage and off. But every now and then, some presenters forget where they are and they, for example, speak dismissively about other presenters or the conference staff in the presence of attendees. Remember that as long as you're at the conference facility, you're on stage.

## Thank the conference director

It's a seemingly small thing, but actually, it's a really big thing. Running a conference is a major job and at times a very challenging one. Take a few moments to locate the conference director, and express your appreciation for the opportunity to present.

Even better, send a thank you note afterwards. These people aren't used to being thanked by presenters. Let them know you appreciate their efforts.

**To recap**

If you've already presented at conferences, everything in this chapter is familiar to you (with the possible except of someone running off with your power cord). If you've yet to give your first conference presentation, I encourage you to give conferences a try. And when you do:

- Meet the deadlines you're given.
- Show up early enough to handle any surprises.
- Watch your gear as you set up.
- Chat with audience members.
- Accept that some people may walk out of your session.
- Repeat each question before you respond to it.
- Behave as if you're on stage even when you're off stage.
- Thank the conference director for the opportunity to present.

**In conclusion**

Increasingly, online conferences are being offered in which all the presenters are presenting remotely and from different locations, and all the attendees are, well, wherever they are. But the popularity of in-person conferences remains strong. This is good news since conferences are an ideal setting for gaining experience in everything from developing new material to responding to unexpected questions. And every conference session you attend as an audience member is an opportunity to gain ideas about what to do, or avoid doing, to advance your presentation expertise.

# CHAPTER 23: PRESENTING WEBINARS

Enabled by Web wizardry and slashed training and travel budgets, webinars have become very popular, especially because many are available at minimal or no charge. That makes webinars an excellent training resource.

When you present a webinar, audience members can be anywhere. They view your slides on their computer screen and hear your presentation via their computer speakers or by dialing into a specified phone number. This chapter will help you prepare and deliver your first (or next) webinar.

## Webinar positives and negatives

For presenters, webinars have both positives and negatives. On the negative side, presenting a webinar is impersonal. You can't see your audience, so you can't gauge how you're doing. You can't have a lively debate with your audience. You present while staring at your computer screen. Of course, for some technical professionals, these may be positives! But if you love interacting with your audience, as I do, webinars may not be your favorite way to present.

Offsetting these negatives is a major positive: you can reach a large audience – more than 500 people in some of the webinars that I've presented – without anyone having to travel. Geography is no constraint on who can attend. People from across Europe, the US, and Canada have all attended some of my webinars. Actually, people from all over the world can attend the same webinar if some are willing to drag themselves to their computers in the middle of the night!

### How to prepare a successful webinar

**Familiarize yourself with the webinar service you'll be using.** For example, review how to access the service, upload your slides, advance your slides, use the drawing tools, and handle questions, so you won't face surprises at show time. Webinar services have a wide and rapidly growing set of capabilities, and no two services are identical. Do a Web search for *webinar services* for some background.

**Make your slides appealing**. Since you're not face-to-face with your audience, your slides take on added importance. To hold people's attention, minimize the use of bullet points, incorporate images, use color and animation, and if appropriate, look for ways you can use the drawing tools, such as the highlighter to emphasize a key point as you talk about it. Plan to move from slide to slide often enough to vary what people are looking at; I aim for a new slide at least every two minutes.

**Ignore the tiny-type rule**. The problem of people being unable to see fine detail at an in-person presentation is less of an issue in webinars because people are viewing the slides right at their computer terminals. As a result, detailed charts, diagrams and the like are easier to see – though it's still unwise to pack slides with border-to-border text.

**Incorporate stories.** Most of the stories you use in your in-person presentations will work fine in a webinar. Just omit or modify those that rely on people seeing your gestures, facial expressions, or body language.

**Conduct a poll**. With most webinar services, you can ask attendees to respond to a multiple choice question, and then display the results for everyone to see. For example, when I present my webinar on introversion and extraversion, I run a poll to find out how many attendees view themselves as introverts and how many as extraverts.

**Keep water handy**. Unless you incorporate a lot of Q&A or other interaction with attendees, you'll be speaking nearly nonstop for the duration of the webinar. You're likely to become dry, so drink as you need to.

**Place all relevant material within easy reach**. In addition to water, make sure you have easy access to whatever else you'll need, such as notes and books you want to refer to. I keep a printout of my slides nearby as a reminder of what slides are coming up.

**Coordinate with the moderator**. Many webinars have a moderator whose responsibilities include such things as welcoming attendees, making sure the webinar starts on time, introducing the presenter, monitoring the webinar as it progresses, and asking the presenter questions that arrived via the chat box. If you'll have a moderator, decide in advance how you'll divide responsibilities. For example, will the moderator introduce you or will you introduce yourself? Do you want to hold questions until the end or respond to them at designated points during the webinar?

## How to deliver a successful webinar

**Take steps to prevent interruptions**. Turn off your cell phone. Close your door (if you're fortunate enough to have a door) to prevent people from dropping in. If you work in a home office, make sure your kids will be elsewhere for the duration. Dogs and cats love to participate in webinars; don't let them.

**Minimize anxiety**. Jeff Switzer, an application software testing professional, and I have discussed how we sometimes feel nervous before presenting a webinar even though we can't see our audience. But that, we concluded, is what causes our nervousness: not being able to connect with the audience or see their reactions. To minimize anxiety, prepare as you would for any other presentation. Be online and ready to start at least 15 minutes before your scheduled start time. Picture a friend or colleague in the audience. Take a deep breath and begin.

**Maintain a pleasant demeanor**. Some webinar services offer a video capability which enables people to see you via a webcam on your computer. If you use this option, be aware of your facial expression; people may be able to see you not only during the webinar, but for several minutes before it starts and after it ends.

**Speak with enthusiasm**. Useful material won't compensate for a sleep-inducing delivery. Many attendees will be doing other things while they listen to you. Present so as to hold their attention. Just as in a telephone conversation, listeners can tell when you're smiling while speaking.

**If you start late, apologize.** I once attended a webinar that started 25 minutes late due to technical problems. When the webinar finally began, the presenter said nothing to indicate she was aware of the delay. Interestingly, the presenter was a professor of communication and she was speaking on communication skills!

**Get to the point quickly.** People are busy. They have neither the time nor the patience for a leisurely approach to the key points. Begin with your objectives and why your topic is important. Then get on with it.

**Present, don't sell.** Unless the stated purpose of the webinar is to sell, don't deliver a sales pitch. People attend webinars for education and information. If you annoy them with sales pitches, they won't hesitate to sign off and they won't return for your subsequent webinars.

**Answer questions concisely.** During a webinar, attendees can submit questions via a chat box and you can respond at intervals or at the end, whichever you prefer. Alternatively, some webinar services allow attendees to ask questions directly, just as in an in-person presentation. However you take questions, keep your responses brief so that you can address several in the time available.

**Invite attendees to contact you afterwards.** Inviting them to send you their questions builds your reputation as a presenter. Very few people actually take you up on this offer, so don't worry; you won't have to spend the rest of your life responding to questions.

**Provide access to your slides.** This enables attendees to review your information and share it with their colleagues. If possible, provide more than just the slides. For example, in addition to a pdf copy of my slides, I like to provide articles on the webinar topic, worksheets, and other related information, as well as discounts on my books and e-books.

**End on time**. Just as in all other presentations, even if you start late, it's still your responsibility to end on time. I give the communication professor credit for ending her one-hour webinar on time despite beginning 25 minutes late.

## To recap

Webinars are an ultra-convenient means of communicating useful information to people who want that information. Most of the guidelines that apply to in-person presentations, such as exhibiting enthusiasm, incorporating stories, and ending on time, apply as well to webinars.

The main difference, aside from the use of technology as a delivery medium (which should pose no problems for most technical professionals), is that you can't see your audience. And that you should close your door (if you have one) to prevent interruptions from your co-workers, kids, or pets. Presentation anxiety is just as normal in presenting a webinar as presenting an in-person presentation – and in both, you improve with experience.

## In conclusion

Keep an eye on how webinars evolve. With the growth of two-way streaming video, which allows for live interaction, impersonal webinar presentations may soon be a thing of the past. To learn more, do a Web search for *webinars* and *two-way streaming video.*

# CHAPTER 24: PRESENTING WITH CO-PRESENTERS

A presentation that you give with co-presenters can deliver more value than you can deliver alone – or less. The experience of presenting with co-presenters can be exhilarating – or debilitating. Your presentation anxiety can be diminished when you present with co-presenters – or amplified. Which of these it turns out to be depends on how you and your co-presenters prepare and share the platform. This chapter offers suggestions to help you do so successfully.

## Co-presenting: a team effort

During a presentation I gave with my colleague, Jackson, he frequently interrupted with comments when it was my turn to present, distracting me and interfering with my flow.

When it was his turn, I kept silent. Afterwards, two people said I seemed awfully quiet when Jackson was presenting. A third asked if I was feeling all right. That's when I realized that the audience perceived the entire session as a joint presentation, with each of us offering comments and questions when the other was the lead.

Thus enlightened, I became more flexible in subsequent presentations with Jackson. Instead of viewing us as giving alternating solo presentations, I came to see us as rotating responsibilities as lead presenter and fellow contributor, and I actively participated when Jackson was the lead. With this change in mindset, I enjoyed our joint presentations much more. So did our audiences.

When you present with others, you share the responsibility for making sure the audience sees the presentation as a team effort. As Fiona Charles, a software testing consultant, explains, "Effective collaborations occur between people who bring different – and complementary – skills, knowledge, and expertise to the presentation."

For example, in one of Fiona's experiential tutorials on business risk for testers, she focused on the practical side, leading exercises, telling stories from her own experience, and soliciting participants' experiences. Her co-presenter's contribution was more theoretical and entailed background reading in preparation. During the tutorial, he led some of the discussions and made sure they captured important points for the group to discuss.

The result: their roles complemented each other, they contributed equally, and their session was a success.

**Prerequisites to co-presenting**

In my experience, the most important factor in presenting with others is trust. In the absence of trust, you have to stay on guard, unsure of what your partners might say. If you trust each other, you can relax, let things flow, and enjoy yourself.

Trust alone is not enough, however. Before you agree to co-present, try to find an opportunity to see your potential partner present, so you can feel comfortable that your styles will mesh. Otherwise, you may face snags, such as I once did when my eagerness to present with a colleague, Lonnie, led me to ignore my own advice.

During our presentation, participants responded in an unexpected way to one of our exercises, taking things in an altogether different direction from what we had anticipated. I was delighted by this surprising twist. Lonnie, however, became stymied – almost paralyzed – by this change in direction. I ended up running the rest of the session.

Fiona Charles suggests that before collaborating with anyone, you discuss your working style to ensure you respect each other and can accommodate the differences in your styles. She emphasizes that the session won't be nearly as good if you don't work on achieving compatibility with your co-presenter. For example, as an introvert, she knows that collaborating with an extravert can be a frustrating experience. But when you are open and honest with each other, it can be an energizing experience for the presenters *and* the audience.

In certain situations, of course, the experience can be delicate, such as when you're co-presenting with customers. That was the case when I was asked to give a presentation to an IT organization to describe the service level agreements I had helped the organization create. Just one problem. I was asked to co-present with Remmy, one of the people on the implementation team.

Remmy was a nice, hard-working guy, but unpopular with his IT co-workers due to his slow, plodding nature and his vague explanations. Consistent with his personality, he was a slow, plodding, vague presenter. I found myself in the awkward position of having to clarify points that he muddled, fill in gaps in his explanations, and demonstrate that at least one of us was neither slow, nor plodding, nor vague. Sometimes, you just have to do the best you can.

## Succeeding with presentation partners

Here are some tips for working with co-presenters:

**Work as a team to plan the content and format**. What will each of you present and for how long? Who will do what, and by when, in preparing the presentation? When will you get together to work on the presentation?

**Determine who will lead each segment**. Make sure you've specified how you'll know when each of you is done and ready to transition to the other.

**If you'll be using slides, decide whether you'll prepare them individually or together**. If individually, determine the format you will each follow so that the slides have a consistent appearance.

**Develop signals you can use during the presentation**. For example, you might want a signal to determine who will take the lead in responding to a question or a signal to indicate that you're stuck and need help.

**Practice together**. You won't know how you'll function together until you try it. Pay particular attention to your timing and your transitions from one to another. Ideally, when each of you is presenting, the other(s) can monitor the audience and detect if any problems are surfacing.

**After the presentation, review what transpired.** What worked? What didn't? What might you do the same or differently next time? It's best, though, not to debrief immediately after the presentation. If things went well, you might be too enthused to be objective about how you can improve. More importantly, if problems emerged, you'd be wise to give yourself some time before critiquing the effort. This applies to all presentations, but may be more important when each of you has had some responsibility for the success of the presentation.

**To recap**

Presenting with partners is a team effort that works best if you trust each other. You need to decide what you're going to do individually and together, both in preparing for the presentation and in delivering it. Most importantly, you need to determine how you're going to collaborate in a way that maintains respect for each of your presentation styles. By functioning as a team, you will enjoy the presentation and your audience will benefit.

**In conclusion**

One of the benefits of a shared presentation is that audience members can experience different styles. And you and your co-presenters can learn from each other's styles. That makes it a win–win undertaking.

# FINAL THOUGHTS

Gayle, a participant in one of my presentation skills workshops, wrote this comment in her evaluation form: "I wish we had spent more time on getting rid of presentation anxiety."

Wouldn't it be wonderful if merely discussing presentation anxiety would make it go away? But Gayle knew that just talking about it isn't enough because she added, "I guess it would have helped if I had given a presentation when you gave us the chance."

Yes, indeed. Two of the class assignments gave participants the opportunity to create a 90-second presentation and then, if they chose to, deliver it. Both times, Gayle opted out.

Contrast Gayle's experience with Bonnie's. Bonnie was terrified of presenting. She told me she just couldn't face it even though being able to present would significantly expand her career opportunities.

Nevertheless, she summoned the courage and attended one of my workshops. The final assignment was to create a presentation of up to two minutes and then, optionally, to give it. Bonnie waited until several others had presented and then, despite her jitters, she presented hers.

Did she fall on her face? No, not even close. Considering that she had only just created the presentation, she did remarkably well. What she was capable of was so much more than she had imagined. Sure, her voice quivered at first, she stumbled over a few thoughts, and there were numerous technical details that could use improvement, but she was fully capable of giving a presentation. She just needed to see it for herself.

Here's the thing. You can learn a lot about presenting by listening to advice, reading books, and observing presenters in action. But you can't learn to present – or learn to present better – by these methods alone. If you want to become a proficient presenter, you have to present.

Giving successful presentations is a skill, and like any other skill, it takes preparation, practice, and persistence. You have to work at it. When you work at it, you get better. And better. And better.

Being able to present well is a huge accomplishment that can be a stepping stone to your future. I encourage you to build those skills, whether through formal classes, Toastmasters meetings (*www.toastmasters.org*), coaching, or any other way that works for you. Seek opportunities to speak at professional association meetings, conferences, and company meetings.

If you have questions about presenting, please contact me at *naomi@nkarten.com*. You tell me your stories and I'll tell you mine. We can learn from each other and have a few laughs about our zany presentation experiences.

You've been a great audience. I wish you many sparkling presentations. Thanks for attending. ☺

# BIBLIOGRAPHY

This bibliography lists all the books I've referenced as well as some others you may find helpful in strengthening your presentation proficiency.

Cliff Atkinson, *Beyond Bullet Points: Using Microsoft® PowerPoint® to Create Presentations That Inform, Motivate, and Inspire*, Microsoft Press, 2005, ISBN 978-0-735620-52-0

Eric Bloom, *Manager Mechanics*, Capital Book, 2006, ISBN 978-1-933102-31-3

Diane DiResta, *Knockout Presentations: How to Deliver Your Message with Power, Punch and Pizzazz*, Chandler House Press, 1998, ISBN 978-1-886284-25-8

Nancy Duarte, *slide:ology: The Art and Science of Creating Great Presentations*, O'Reilly Media, Inc., 2008, ISBN 978-0-596522-34-6

Jutta Eckstein. *Agile Software Development in the Large. Diving into the Deep*, Dorset House Publishing, 2004, ISBN 978-0-932633-57-6

Michael Erard, *Um...: Slips, Stumbles, and Verbal Blunders, and What They Mean*, Anchor, 2008, ISBN 978-1-400095-43-8

W. Timothy Gallwey, *Inner Skiing. Revised Edition*, Random House, 1997, ISBN 978-0-679778-27-1

Ellen Gottesdiener, *Requirements by Collaboration. Workshops for Defining Needs*, Addison-Wesley, 2002, ISBN 978-0-201786-06-4

# Bibliography

Chip Heath and Dan Heath, *Made to Stick: Why Some Ideas Survive and Others Die*, Random House, 2007, ISBN 978-1-400064-28-1

Bruce M. Hood, *Supersense: Why We Believe in the Unbelievable*, HarperOne, 2009, ISBN 978-0-061452-64-2

Naomi Karten, *Changing How You Manage and Communicate Change: Focusing on the Human Side of Change*, IT Governance Publishing, 2009, ISBN 978-1-905356-94-2

Naomi Karten, *How to Survive, Excel and Advance as an Introvert*, Karten Associates, 2006

Naomi Karten, *Managing Expectations: Working with People Who Want More, Better, Faster, Sooner, NOW!*, Dorset House Publishing, 1994, ISBN 978-0-932633-27-9

Naomi Karten, *Perceptions & Realities* newsletter, posted at *www.nkarten.com/newslet.html*, ISSN 1079-5952

Timothy J. Koegel, *The Exceptional Presenter*, Greenleaf Group Book Press, 2007, ISBN 978-1-929774-44-9

Malcolm Kushner, *Presentations for Dummies*, Wiley Publishing, Inc., 2004, ISBN 978-0-764559-55-6

Randy Olson, *Don't Be Such a Scientist: Talking Substance in an Age of Style*, Island Press, 2009. ISBN 978-1-597265-63-8

Drew Provan, *Giving Great Presentations in Easy Steps*, In Easy Steps Limited, 2009, ISBN 978-1-840783-71-1

Garr Reynolds, *Presentation Zen: Simple Ideas on Presentation Design and Delivery*, New Riders, 2008, ISBN 978-0-321525-65-9

# Bibliography

Johanna Rothman, *Manage Your Project Portfolio: Increase Your Capacity and Finish More Projects*, Pragmatic Bookshelf, 2009, ISBN 978-1-934356-29-6

Lou Russell, *10 Steps to Successful Project Management*, ASTD Press, 2007, ISBN 978-1-562864-63-7

Doug Stevenson, *Doug Stevenson's Story Theater Method: Strategic Storytelling in Business*, Cornelia Press, 2008, ISBN 978-0-977914-61-6

Chic Thompson, *What a Great Idea! 2.0: Unlocking Your Creativity in Business and in Life*, Sterling, 2007, ISBN 978-1-402741-88-3

Edward R. Tufte, *The Cognitive Style of PowerPoint: Pitching Out Corrupts Within, Second Edition*, Graphics Press, 2006, ISBN 978-0-961392-16-1

Edward R. Tufte, *The Visual Display of Quantitative Information, Second Edition*, Graphics Press, 2001, ISBN 978-0-961392-14-7

Claudyne Wilder, *Point, Click & Wow! The Habits and Techniques of Successful Presenters*, Pfeiffer, 2008, ISBN 978-0-787997-45-8

# ITG RESOURCES

IT Governance Ltd. sources, creates and delivers products and services to meet the real-world, evolving IT governance needs of today's organizations, directors, managers, and practitioners. The ITG website (*www.itgovernance.co.uk*) is the international one-stop shop for corporate and IT governance information, advice, guidance, books, tools, training, and consultancy.

*www.itgovernance.co.uk/catalog/715* is the category page on our website that gives details all of our soft skills titles.

**Other websites**

Books and tools published by IT Governance Publishing (ITGP) are available from all business booksellers and are also immediately available from the following websites:

*www.itgovernance.co.uk/catalog/355* provides information and online purchasing facilities for every currently available book published by ITGP.

*www.itgovernanceusa.com* is a US$-based website that delivers the full range of IT Governance products to North America, and ships from within the continental US.

*www.itgovernanceasia.com* provides a selected range of ITGP products specifically for customers in South Asia.

*www.27001.com* is the IT Governance Ltd. website that deals specifically with information security management, and ships from within the continental US.

## Pocket guides

For full details of the entire range of pocket guides, simply follow the links at *www.itgovernance.co.uk/publishing.aspx*.

## Toolkits

ITG's unique range of toolkits includes the IT Governance Framework Toolkit, which contains all the tools and guidance that you will need in order to develop and implement an appropriate IT governance framework for your organisation. Full details can be found at *www.itgovernance.co.uk/products/519*.

For a free paper on how to use the proprietary Calder-Moir IT Governance Framework, and for a free trial version of the toolkit, see *www.itgovernance.co.uk/calder_moir.aspx*.

There is also a wide range of toolkits to simplify implementation of management systems, such as an ISO/IEC 27001 ISMS or a BS25999 BCMS, and these can all be viewed and purchased online at *www.itgovernance.co.uk/catalog/1*.

## Best Practice Reports

ITG's range of Best Practice Reports is now at *www.itgovernance.co.uk/best-practice-reports.aspx*. These offer you essential, pertinent, expertly researched information on an increasing number of key issues including Web 2.0 and Green IT.

## Training and consultancy

IT Governance also offers training and consultancy services across the entire spectrum of disciplines in the information governance arena. Details of training courses can be accessed at *www.itgovernance.co.uk/training.aspx* and descriptions of our consultancy services can be found at *www.itgovernance.co.uk/consulting.aspx*. Why not contact us to see how we could help you and your organisation?

**Newsletter**

IT governance is one of the hottest topics in business today, not least because it is also the fastest moving, so what better way to keep up than by subscribing to ITG's free monthly newsletter *Sentinel*? It provides monthly updates and resources across the whole spectrum of IT governance subject matter, including risk management, information security, ITIL and IT service management, project governance, compliance and so much more. Subscribe for your free copy at *www.itgovernance.co.uk/newsletter.aspx*.

CPSIA information can be obtained at www.ICGtesting.com
Printed in the USA
BVOW07s1131120813

328218BV00001B/23/P